JEREMY O. HARRIS

Jeremy O. Harris's full-length plays include *Slave Play* (New York Theatre Workshop, *New York Times* Critics' Pick, Winner of the 2018 Kennedy Center Rosa Parks Playwriting Award, the Lorraine Hansberry Playwriting Award, and the Lotos Foundation Prize in the Arts and Sciences); *"Daddy"* (Vineyard Theatre/The New Group); *Xander Xyst, Dragon: 1*; and *WATER SPORTS; or insignificant white boys* (published by 53rd State Press). His work has been presented or developed by Pieter Space, JACK, Ars Nova, The New Group, NYTW, Performance Space New York, and Playwrights Horizons. In 2018, Jeremy co-wrote A24's upcoming film *Zola* with director Janicza Bravo. He is the recipient of the Vineyard Theatre's Paula Vogel Playwrighting Award; he is a 2016 MacDowell Colony Fellow, an Orchard Project Greenhouse artist, and a resident playwright with Colt Coeur. He is under commission from Lincoln Center Theater and Playwrights Horizons. Jeremy received an MFA from the Yale School of Drama.

Jeremy O. Harris

"DADDY"
A Melodrama

NICK HERN BOOKS
London
www.nickhernbooks.co.uk

A Nick Hern Book

"Daddy" first published in Great Britain in 2022 as a paperback original by Nick Hern Books Limited, The Glasshouse, 49a Goldhawk Road, London W12 8QP

"Daddy" copyright © 2022 Jeremy O. Harris

Jeremy O. Harris has asserted his moral right to be identified as the author of this work

Front cover image: Dolls designed by Tschabalala Self; photographed by Hsiang Hsi

Back cover image of Terique Jarrett (Franklin) in the 2022 Almeida Theatre production, photographed by Sebastian Nevols; concept by Émilie Chen

Designed and typeset by Nick Hern Books, London
Printed in the UK by Mimeo Ltd, Huntingdon, Cambridgeshire PE29 6XX

A CIP catalogue record for this book is available from the British Library

ISBN 978 1 83904 087 0

"Daddy" received its world premiere as a co-production between The New Group and Vineyard Theatre, at The New Group, New York City, on 13 February 2019, with the following cast:

FRANKLIN	Ronald Peet
ANDRE	Alan Cumming
MAX	Tommy Dorfman
BELLAMY	Kahyun Kim
ZORA	Charlayne Woodard
ALESSIA	Hari Nef
GOSPEL CHOIR	Carrie Compere
	Denise Manning
	Onyie Nwachukwu

Director	Danya Taymor
Set Designer	Matt Saunders
Co-Costume Designers	Montana Levi Blanco
Lighting Designer	Isabella Byrd
Sound Designer	Lee Kinney
Hair, Wig and Make-up Designer	Cookie Jordan
Original Score and Arrangements	Lee Kinney
Original Vocal Music and Arrangements	Darius Smith and Brett Macias
Music Supervisor	Brett Macias
Intimacy and Fight Director	Claire Warden
Movement Director	Darrell Grand Moultrie
Doll Designer	Tschabalala Self

The play received its British premiere at the Almeida Theatre, London, on 26 March 2022, with the following cast:

FRANKLIN	Terique Jarrett
ANDRE	Claes Bang
MAX	John McCrea
BELLAMY	Ioanna Kimbook
ZORA	Sharlene Whyte
ALESSIA	Jenny Rainsford
GOSPEL CHOIR	Rebecca Bernice Amissah
	Keisha Atwell
	T'Shan Williams

Director	Danya Taymor
Set Designer	Matt Saunders
Co-Costume Designers	Montana Levi Blanco
	and Peter Todd
Lighting Designer	Isabella Byrd
Sound Designer and	
* Original Music*	Lee Kinney
Music Supervisor	Tim Sutton
Original Vocal Score	Darius Smith
Hair and Make-up	
* Designer*	Cynthia De La Rosa
Choreographer/	
* Movement Director*	Anjali Mehra
Intimacy and Fight	
* Director*	Yarit Dor
Casting Director	Amy Ball
Doll Designer	Tschabalala Self
Dialect Coach	Brett Tyne
Costume Supervisor	Olivia Ward
Assistant Director	Mumba Dodwell

For Mama + Granny who kept The Word close and me closer.
You were my light whenever the world tried to pull me into the
dark.

For Ross for seeing this and me…

For Mitchel Civello for telling me I wasn't done and forcing me
to rewrite it till it was. For believing in me the way only a best
friend can.

He live in a palace,
bought me Alexander McQueen
he was keeping me stylish...
I'm high as hell, I only took a half a pill.
I'm on some dumb shit.

Nicki Minaj, 'Anaconda'

...there's the bizarre fact that queerness reads,
even to some black gay men themselves, as a
kind of whiteness. In a black, Christian-informed
culture, where relatively few men head
households anymore, whiteness is equated with
perversity, a pollutant further eroding the already
decimated black family.

Hilton Als, *White Girls*

Characters

FRANKLIN, *mid-twenties. Black. An artist. Has the slightest hint of a Southern accent, becomes subtly pronounced as the play progresses*

ANDRE, *fifties to sixties. White. One of those possibly ethnic Europeans with the unmistakable accent of the incredibly wealthy. A collector who buys art with an explicit worth*

MAX, *mid-twenties. White. Franklin's best friend. Looks great in a swimsuit. An actor who has been cast as a lead in three network pilots that weren't picked up. This is the first time he's been in a play*

BELLAMY, *mid-twenties. A Non-Black WOC. Looks better in a swimsuit. She's quite happy with her own directionlessness. She has 9.3K Instagram followers*

ZORA, *forties to sixties, Black. Franklin's mother. Someone who sees the world as it is and not how she wishes it were. A Virginian and a soldier for Christ*

ALESSIA, *any age. A gallerist who is sharp and direct. Which is rare, I gather*

GOSPEL CHOIR, *Franklin's forgotten heart and soul*

Setting

90077 (Bel Air, Los Angeles, California).

Time

Now.

Notes on Style

Google David Hockney's "Portrait of an Artist (Pool with Two Figures)" 1971, if you've never seen it. Also, I listened to a lot of George Michael, Nicki Minaj and Shirley Caesar while writing.

The intimacy in the play should feel real in all its forms. All the action of the play takes place in, around and about Andre's pool.

Everybody talks but no one listens. Have fun with that.

Things said in parentheses are sort of spoken secrets, unconscious truths. A (/) in the text indicates that the next line of dialogue should begin.

Also, although I used visual descriptors of the characters in this play that may lead you to believe I want a cast of "pretty" people, note: THIS PLAY'S CHARACTERS MUST BE "PRETTY", THE CHARACTERS NOT YOUR PERCEPTION OF THE ACTORS. THERE IS A DIFFERENCE.

When lost, look to melodrama for direction (see: Peter Brooks' *The Melodramatic Imagination*), because this play moves from melodrama's dream to melodrama's nightmare.

Franklin propulsively regresses from Young Man, to Boy, to Baby from act to act until he emerges as himself again. The actor portraying him should luxuriate in this.

ACT ONE (FRANKLIN + ANDRE)

Scene One

*Before us, downstage, there is an expansive infinity pool.
Perhaps there are inflatables? Perhaps not. Upstage there are
five poolside chaise lounges.*

*Behind those, a glass wall and a sliding door leading to a stark
white room that may or may not have art on the walls. When the
door is slid closed you can't hear what's being said behind it.*

FRANKLIN *stands in the middle of the room looking around.
He is dripping wet and wearing only a Speedo. He's a bit more
than drunk.*

ANDRE *enters with a towel. He's touching himself, his face,
high on molly. The sliding door is open.*

ANDRE. How was the pool?

FRANKLIN. Is that a Twombly?

ANDRE. You know him?

FRANKLIN. Obsessed.
    Saw his, um,
    his retrospective last year.
    I got lost in all the swirls.

ANDRE. (Goddamn you're beautiful.)
    Was that –
    It was molly / you gave me right?

FRANKLIN. Did you know Rauschenberg left his wife for
    Twombly?
    I didn't –
    so random...
    just,
    yeah...

I think it was molly
unless it was K…

Pause.

There was this old white lady
who DID NOT
approve of that fact
being in the audio tour.

ANDRE (*reaching out for* FRANKLIN*'s legs*). Has anyone ever
     told you
     you have legs like Naomi?

FRANKLIN. Naomi?

ANDRE. Campbell.
     She also did a lap in my pool once.

     A moment…

FRANKLIN. Oh.
     No.
     Nobody's ever said that.

     …
     (Fuck.
     I'm super high.)

ANDRE. May I?

     FRANKLIN *gestures that he may.*

     ANDRE *begins to rub his face up and down* FRANKLIN*'s
     legs.*

     From his feet to his thighs.

     (*Still rubbing.*) (Mmmm…
     Smooth.
     Like the sweetest chocolate.)

FRANKLIN.…
     You know…
     The woman,
     that white woman from the retrospective,
     she kept saying,

"Why?"
Over and over...
"Why?"
Then she was like,
"Why do they INSIST on shoving it down our throats.
The man,
he paints,
I don't give a rat's ass if he was sleeping with Big Foot!
Just tell me about the goddamn paintings.
You know?
It's just –
Everything else?
It's all just gossip.
And I do NOT respond well to gossip.
I don't take it from my children and I don't take it from my friends
and I DO NOT want to be forced to engage with it at a museum exhibition."
Then her little group of rich white lady friends,
definitely members,
maybe donors,
sort of shook their heads in agreement and took off their little earphones.
Then walked away.
...

He begins to laugh.

That tickles.

ANDRE (*he continues rubbing*). Do you know a lot about art?

FRANKLIN. A bit...
I'm an artist, or
Whatever...
I actually have a like
just like a little show /
coming up in a –

ANDRE. Amazing.
You know
I have more.
All the best.

FRANKLIN *moves a bit away, looking around.*

FRANKLIN. I saw the Calder in your living room.
And there was a Lichtenstein in your foyer.

ANDRE (*a come-on*) And an O'Keeffe in the kitchen.
An Arbus
and two Shermans in my office.

FRANKLIN....

...

...

ANDRE (*standing up*). But you haven't seen my favorite room
yet.

ANDRE *grabs* FRANKLIN*'s arm and stares into his face
deeply. It's weird but it has a sort of creepy sensuality to it,
European.*

FRANKLIN. What's so special about it?

ANDRE. See for yourself.
Go through that door
take an immediate left
then open the first door on the right.

FRANKLIN *looks at him for a moment and then walks out
of the room.* ANDRE *rubs his own face for a few moments
and smiles.*

*There is the sound of someone excitedly running down a
hallway before* FRANKLIN *re-enters.*

FRANKLIN *has a new light in his eyes.*

FRANKLIN. You have a room full of BASQUIATS?

ANDRE. I loaned a few to SFMOMA
but yeah.

FRANKLIN. This is –

FRANKLIN *starts to laugh now. Struck by the absurdity of
it all.*

ANDRE. Little Naomi.
You're so...

Look at you. /
Goddamn.

FRANKLIN. Don't you find that a bit gauche?

ANDRE. What?

FRANKLIN. A room full of Basquiats?
    Don't get me wrong it's
    like,
    it's cool,
    Like,
    Amazing... or whatever.
    But it's
    Like, yeah,
    you have money but
    curatorially
    the taste is like,
    booty.

ANDRE. Booty?

FRANKLIN. Yeah.
    Like,
    straight
    ass.
    The pieces in that room are essentially in conversations with
    each other.
    Which is so boring.
    A Basquiat can't be in conversation with itself.
    It has to be...
    like...
    like, Basquiat is such a big personality.
    There can only ever really be
    like
    one of him in a room at a time.
    Otherwise the space gets overwhelmed.

ANDRE. Interesting...

FRANKLIN. Also,
    don't you think,
    like,
    well like, owning a Calder

like a big Calder
is also gauche.
Especially
when you have like…
a Sherman in your office
And an Arbus in the bathroom?
(ugh…)

ANDRE *smiles and begins to walk around* FRANKLIN
taking stock of his body like he's a sculpture ripe for
procurement, except this is a statue he can touch when he
sees an imperfection, a perfection.

ANDRE. My interior architect
    didn't think so.

FRANKLIN. Your interior architect either has bad taste
    or wanted their fee to be higher.
    Because right now you seem like the kind of dude who has a
    shit ton of money,
    But like,
    No guidance,
    no education
    and no taste.
    Like, this screams nouveau riche.
    You know?

FRANKLIN *looks at* ANDRE *and realizes he's drunk.*

    Oh.
    Fuck. I'm sorry.
    (goddamn it.
    goddman it.
    goddamn.)

ANDRE. Why are you apologizing?

FRANKLIN. Because I have this
    like
    habit?
    Of like –
    trying to force everyone to see
    the world how I see it?
    So,

like
I can't shut up
sometimes
I just like
say and say and say and say
everything I've ever thought
like it matters to anyone besides me.

ANDRE *stands face to face with* FRANKLIN *and looks at him, daring him to flinch.*

FRANKLIN *looks back and in an instant* ANDRE*'s tongue is taking a deep dive into his slightly agape mouth. Their tongues swim together like synchronized swimmers in an Olympic meet.*

ANDRE (*pulling away and grabbing his face*). Be mine.

FRANKLIN. What?

ANDRE. I want you.
      You... uh
      Ha
      You're –
      …
      …
      Tell me what I should I get.
      Let me see the world like you.

FRANKLIN. What?

ANDRE. If you were me.
      What would you buy?
      Who should I have on these walls?
      …
      …
      You?
      …
      …
      Tell me
      and it's here.
      Curate.
      You have a show coming up…
      Should I populate the walls with your stuff?

FRANKLIN....
     Stop it.

ANDRE. I'm serious.
     Should I?

FRANKLIN. No.

ANDRE. Why not?

FRANKLIN. Because...
     art...
     art loses its worth
     the minute it can be bought?
     or like...
     yeah...
     It becomes worthless
     once it's owned.

     ANDRE *grabs* FRANKLIN*'s face and pulls it close to his –*
     nuzzling temple to temple.

     They stay there for a long moment, ANDRE *looking deeply*
     into FRANKLIN.

ANDRE. Just...
     Stay here.
     Talk to me tonight.
     Say and say and say to me
     until you slip up and say something you never thought you'd
     think.

     The opening synth notes to George Michael's 1988 #1 hit
     single "Father Figure" begin to play.

     FRANKLIN *looks up, almost aware (in that way the drunk*
     or the high can almost peer into those dimensions that run
     parallel to their own if only for a moment) that his life is
     being scored.

FRANKLIN. Um...
     ...
     ...
     ...
     ...
     uh...

...
...
...
Ok?

A GOSPEL CHOIR *from far off begins to sing.*

He reaches out to kiss ANDRE *again just as the first verse is on the verge of beginning.*

Scene Two

FRANKLIN *lays by the pool with* MAX *and* BELLAMY. *He is wearing the same Speedo as before, he now has on a pair of brand new Gucci sunglasses.*

They are passing a vial of cocaine back and forth throughout as they drink mimosas.

MAX. Where did you meet him?

FRANKLIN. After the Night Gallery show
    At that new spot.

MAX. Which one?

FRANKLIN. The really good one.
    The one where you have to enter through a kitchen.

MAX. Oh P & A.

FRANKLIN. No the other one.

MAX. Oh yeah FKT.

FRANKLIN. FKT is closed now.

MAX. PFC Pleasure Factory?

FRANKLIN. Yes!
    Maybe...?
    I don't remember.
    I was super high.

MAX. Fuck.
  Why didn't you invite me?

FRANKLIN. I did.
  You said you were busy
  with Marcus.

MAX. Fuck Marcus.

BELLAMY. Franklin…
  Are those the new Guccis?

MAX. Oh my god they are!

BELLAMY. Shut up!
  I want the new Guccis!

FRANKLIN. He got them for me yesterday.

MAX. What the fuck…

FRANKLIN. I know…

MAX. You hit the jackpot.

FRANKLIN. It's not like that.

BELLAMY. Can I try them on?
  I love Gucci.
  Alessandro is bae.

MAX. He's a troll isn't he?
  Plying you with gifts and shit.

BELLAMY. No judgments…
  I'd let a troll fuck me for Gucci.

FRANKLIN (*laughing*). No.
  He's like super hot.

MAX. How hot?

FRANKLIN. I don't know…
  Why does / it matter?

MAX. Troll

BELLAMY (*laughing*). Totally.

FRANKLIN. No.

He's hot. You just…
It's like…
it's like,
my whole world shifts when he looks at me.
And like
everything I could ever conceive
is the epitome of conception.

There's a moment… FRANKLIN *feeling* ANDRE's *eyes.*

BELLAMY. Oh my god, that's beautiful.

MAX. That's… so gay.
What does he do?

FRANKLIN. What?
I don't know.
He just sort of has money.

MAX. Well,
that's the hottest thing you've said so far.

BELLAMY. Can I please try on the Guccis?

FRANKLIN *hands them over. She holds them as though
she's been bestowed a tiara and slowly puts them on.*

FRANKLIN. He owns a couple galleries in Thailand.
He says the market is crazy there.
Australians on vacay blow stacks
on artists they've never even heard of.

MAX. Australia is just a continent of rich idiots.

BELLAMY. I love it.
Australia can get it any time.

FRANKLIN. He actually –
well he implied that if I wanted to
like run the Thai gallery it was mine.
So I…
I mean…
(Obviously that's CRAZY.
But I'm thinking about it.)
After my show
I think I'm going to like,
seriously consider something like that.

FRANKLIN *finishes his mimosa. Immediately embarrassed about exposing that:*

Um…
I'm gonna get another one.
You guys good?

MAX. I'll take another.

BELLAMY. I'm good…

FRANKLIN *exits.* BELLAMY *is taking selfies with her iPhone.*

Don't I look AMAZING in these?
Gucci DEFINITELY suits my skin tone.

MAX. Bellamy, this is fucking insane.
How the hell did Franklin
get a goddamn sugar daddy?

BELLAMY. I don't even need to retouch this one.
They look that good.

MAX. I mean
this goes beyond a sugar daddy
this is a fucking sugar despot.
Who is this man?
A fucking Saudi sheik?
My god.

BELLAMY. Do you think he'd let me keep these?
You know since he didn't really pay for them?

MAX. I have to meet this guy.
He's gotta be a troll,
we'd already know about a guy this rich if he were hot.

BELLAMY. You sound crazy Max.

FRANKLIN *re-enters, setting a glass beside* MAX.
FRANKLIN*'s phone begins to ring on the chaise.*

FRANKLIN (*looking at his phone*). Guys feel free to stay over.
Andre told me if I felt lonely I could have friends.
And since you're family you never have to leave.

Pause.

He ignores the call.

MAX (*looking over to* BELLAMY). So crazy he just left you
    here... /
    When does he get back?

FRANKLIN. Well we've been dating for a bit.
    It's not that crazy.

BELLAMY. Franklin?

    BELLAMY *beams at* FRANKLIN *expectantly.*

FRANKLIN. No, Bellamy.
    You can't have them.

BELLAMY. But we're family...

FRANKLIN. I'll get you a pair next week
    when he's back.

BELLAMY. Shut up.

FRANKLIN. I will.

BELLAMY. SHUT
    UP!
    OHMYGOD!
    (*Hugging him deeply.*)
    You're the best.

MAX. Don't you think you're moving too fast?

    FRANKLIN *leaves the hug and looks back at* MAX. *His
    phone begins to ring again.*

FRANKLIN. What?

MAX. I mean...
    dude.
    You like,
    you move in practically
    a SECOND
    after meeting this guy.
    You're like

    FRANKLIN *sees who is calling. Fuck.*

FRANKLIN. No.
    It's not like that –
    It's –

MAX. You haven't mentioned
    your show like, once
    like what are you even
    like what are you working on?
    You know?

FRANKLIN. Um…
    a lot. I think.
    I've figured out. –
    (*Holding up his phone.*)
    This is actually Alessia now…
    Hold on.

    FRANKLIN *gets up and answers the phone. He walks over
    to the sliding door and closes it shut. Behind the glass all we
    see are his lips moving.*

    During this conversation MAX *looks back incredulous,
    attempting to hear what little he can.* BELLAMY *looks at
    her phone, beaming.*

BELLAMY. I'm literally blowing up right now.
    (*Reading a comment.*)
    "You're gorgeous. Die."
    Oh my god everyone is obsessed.

MAX. Shhh.
    Why do you even care?

BELLAMY. Why shouldn't I?

    *They hold each other's gaze for a moment – two siblings
    about to pounce.*

MAX. Bellamy?

BELLAMY. Max?

    …
    …
    You're jealous…

MAX. Bellamy

don't be stupid.
I'm not
like,
jealous of Franklin.

BELLAMY. Max.
I'm not stupid
and I never said you were jealous
of Franklin.
(*She looks back at her phone.*)
The stans are VIOLENT tonight
I love.
"Smother me with your opulence Mama!"
So cute!

BELLAMY *goes back to her phone, responding to her Insta messages as MAX stands up.*

FRANKLIN *walks back out right as MAX gets up and jumps in the pool.*

MAX *looks up at FRANKLIN as he sets his phone down upon the chaise lounge.*

MAX. Everything ok?

FRANKLIN. Just talking about the show.

MAX. Cool.
    …
    …
    Cool.
    …
    …
    Is he the top or the bottom?

FRANKLIN. What?

MAX. Who's fucking who?

BELLAMY. Oh my god,
can you please not this is so annoying.

FRANKLIN (*to MAX*). Why does it matter?

MAX. I don't know
    I'm

I'm just like
curious,
or whatever.

BELLAMY. Ignore him Franklin he's just jealous.

MAX. Jealous has nothing to do with –
What? No. Bellamy? No.
For us? This…
I might as well be asking if he sleeps with his socks on.

FRANKLIN. Max that's so fucking stupid.

MAX. Ok
then tell me.

…
Who's the top?

FRANKLIN *looks at* MAX *for a second before smiling –
emboldening swiftly.*

FRANKLIN (*taking off his Speedo*). It depends on the night.

He stands there for a moment, still feeling ANDRE*'s eyes on
him. Suddenly the* GOSPEL CHOIR *that sounded far off,
seem closer.* FRANKLIN *looks up for a moment as though
faintly hearing.*

He throws his Speedo onto the chaise lounge beside
BELLAMY *and dives into the pool.*

Scene Three

*In darkness, water in the pool flies about in a torrent. There is
the potential of a poolside tsunami and the sounds of subsiding
sex fill the air.*

As the lights rise ANDRE *pushes off from* FRANKLIN *and
backstrokes downstage to the edge of the pool.* FRANKLIN,
*with his arms on the side of the pool downstage, his back to the
audience, sits panting for a moment.*

ANDRE. You ok?

FRANKLIN, *slightly shaking* (*his body navigating the space between pain and pleasure*), *pulls himself from the pool. He walks, naked, to the chaise and lies down.* ANDRE *stares.*

FRANKLIN. I'm good.
　　I'm just…
　　Yeah.
　　That was…
　　Yeah.

There's a moment – just the sound of the water, breathing.

ANDRE.…
　　sometimes looking at you is like a gift.

FRANKLIN.…Thanks?

ANDRE *swims back toward the upstage edge of the pool.*

ANDRE. You ok?

FRANKLIN. Why do you keep asking that?

ANDRE. You just seemed like you weren't as deeply involved as I was.

He throws water onto his face.

FRANKLIN. I was.
　　No.
　　I –
　　I just.

Pause.

　　I haven't done that before.

ANDRE. In a pool?
　　Isn't it the best?
　　The smoothness.
　　It's clean.
　　Like,
　　Like skating on new ice.
　　At least for me,
　　That's always been my feeling.
　　Like there's no end to your body
　　No beginning to mine.
　　Vice versa.

FRANKLIN. Do you think we
  like
  are moving too fast?
  Or something?
  Like.
  You don't even
  know,
  like,
  anything
  about me.
  My show is in
  a month and you
  …
  I don't know.
  You haven't asked me anything about it.

ANDRE. I'm sorry.
  Is that –
  Are you ok?

FRANKLIN. No!
  Yes?
  Fuck…
  ugh
  Like,
  ok,
  I haven't like,
  well,
  like I haven't like,
  been fucked.
  Before.
  so…

  This drops like bricks sinking to the bottom of the pool before
  ANDRE *can react.*

  It was great.
  I just.
  I just haven't done that.
  Yet.
  I hadn't, done that.
  Um,
  Yet.

And I don't even,
like
tell dudes
that I haven't
like,
done that.
Because that can be used
as like
this like
measuring stick?
For your queerness?
Like, if bottoming is hard for you
or you haven't done it
you're like an inferior queer person.
And I don't know…
I just.
ugh.

More silence. ANDRE *gets out of the pool.*

ANDRE. You ok?

FRANKLIN. I just said –
(*He laughs.*)
Yeah!
I'm.
Yeah.
I just need some time.

ANDRE.…
…
…
…
…
…
But you enjoyed yourself.
…
…right?
…

ANDRE *stares down at* FRANKLIN *and begins to speak softly, assertively. It's sexy.*

Do you like me being your teacher?

Do you –
Did you,
Did you like that?

FRANKLIN looks at ANDRE standing over him.

FRANKLIN. Yeah…

ANDRE. You did?
You liked that Naomi?

ANDRE reaches down and begins caressing FRANKLIN's body.

FRANKLIN *(feeling it)*. Yes.
Yes I did.
I do.

ANDRE *(moving his hands quicker now)*. Do you want me to teach you more?

FRANKLIN looks up.

FRANKLIN. Like what?

ANDRE. Like more…

FRANKLIN. I –

Before FRANKLIN can respond ANDRE smacks his bare bottom.

ANDRE. Do you want me to teach you more?

FRANKLIN lets out a laugh. He slaps him again.

FRANKLIN *(laughing)*. I –

ANDRE slaps him again.

ANDRE. No more "I".
Just "yes, sir".
"No, sir".

FRANKLIN. Yes, sir.

ANDRE. You want me to teach you more?

He slaps him again. FRANKLIN lets the pain run up and down his spine. He bites his lip and smiles:

FRANKLIN. Yes sir.

ANDRE *slaps him again, harder this time.*

ANDRE. Good.
Turn around.

FRANKLIN. I –

ANDRE *slaps him again harder.*

ANDRE. What did I say, Naomi?

FRANKLIN. Yes, sir.

FRANKLIN *turns over.*

ANDRE *looks down at him. He surveys his naked body and a smile starts to cross his face.*

He traces his hand over FRANKLIN*'s chest. Getting close to his crotch but never touching it.*

ANDRE. You like this?

FRANKLIN. Yes sir.

He touches more, his hands moving closer to his crotch.

ANDRE. You want me to touch you there?

FRANKLIN. No, sir.

ANDRE (*surprised*). You don't?

FRANKLIN. No, Daddy.

ANDRE *moves his hand abruptly.*

ANDRE. What?

FRANKLIN. What?

ANDRE. What did you just say?

FRANKLIN *looks up, surprised.*

FRANKLIN. No, sir.

ANDRE. What?

FRANKLIN. I said, "No, sir"

ANDRE. No you didn't.
  You said,
  "no Daddy".

  FRANKLIN *looks around*.

FRANKLIN. What?

  Another moment.

ANDRE. Do you want me to be your daddy?

  A perverse pleasure begins moving through the air.

FRANKLIN. No, sir.

ANDRE. Call me Daddy.

FRANKLIN. No sir.

  ANDRE *flips* FRANKLIN *back onto his stomach. He hits him four times hard on his backside.*

ANDRE. Call me Daddy.

FRANKLIN. No, sir.

  ANDRE *hits him again*.

FRANKLIN. Ow, Daddy.

ANDRE. What did you say?

FRANKLIN (*looking up at him*). Ow, Daddy.

  …
  No more.

  ANDRE *reaches down and grabs* FRANKLIN'*s face and licks it.*

ANDRE. Say it again:
  "Daddy."

FRANKLIN. Daddy.

  ANDRE *steps back and looks at him.*

ANDRE. Don't move.
  Stay right there.
  Let me look at you.

He does.

As FRANKLIN *inhales and exhales* ANDRE *watches and absorbs every facet of him as though his body is a meal and his eyes are his mouth.*

ANDRE. Ok.
   …
   …
Now,
tell Daddy what you want him to do.

Pause.

Suddenly the sound of a CHOIR *again, louder, closer, as though coming from all sides, lands upon* FRANKLIN *and his relationship to the space fractures momentarily once again.*

You get the sense, for a collection of moments, that maybe he's peering just beyond his present world into ours.

Then he's back and looking up at ANDRE, *the voice of the* CHOIR *still rising, underscoring the following:*

FRANKLIN. I want Daddy…
I want Daddy to, to put his thumb in my mouth.

He does.

And I want Daddy
I want Daddy to ask me about my show.

ANDRE (*smiling*). You do?

ANDRE's *thumb traces* FRANKLIN's *lips falling in and out of his mouth.*

Tell me about your show, baby.

FRANKLIN (*sucking on* ANDRE's *thumb*). My show…
Well
my show is at Keller Space
it's –
It's a solo show…
And it's a continuation
of my series

of soft sculptures.
The gallerist there, Alessia,
she
she really likes them…
they
are like these weird dolls
of black boys.
Possibly me,
all naked,
deformed,
and,
like
reminiscent of Xavier Roberts' Cabbage Patch Kids
or more precisely
Martha Nelson Thomas'
"Original Doll Babies".
And…
The show evokes a sense of
nostalgia?
While also
like…
well…
(according to the press release)
recontextualizing what it means to be a black man.

The sound of the CHOIR *is gone.* ANDRE *pulls his thumb
out of* FRANKLIN*'s mouth then rubs his head, paternal.*

A moment. He puts his thumb back in.

ANDRE. That…
    yeah…

Pause.

    it sounds lovely Franklin.

FRANKLIN. There's a lot more to it than that too…
    It's like / going to

ANDRE. Let me be surprised.

FRANKLIN. Ok.

    …

ANDRE. It really does sound lovely, Franklin.

FRANKLIN. You think so?

ANDRE. I know so.

Pause.

FRANKLIN. Are you proud of me?

ANDRE. Of course.

FRANKLIN. Of course what?

ANDRE. What?

FRANKLIN. Call me son.

ANDRE....Of course I'm proud of you son.

FRANKLIN....

   ...

   ...I love you.

ANDRE. I love you, son.

   FRANKLIN *takes* ANDRE's *thumb out of his mouth turns onto his back, curls up and giggles. Like Micheal Jackson or a child.*

   He looks up at ANDRE, *earnest.*

FRANKLIN. Really Daddy?

Scene Four

In darkness we hear the sound of a ringtone. The phone rings and rings in its sorrowful way.

Until there is a BEEP!

FRANKLIN (*voice-over*). Hi, you've reached Franklin.
   Sorry I uh,
   I can't get to the phone right now.
   But if you need anything just leave a message
   Or, like, send me an email

or a text
and I'll get back to you at my earliest convenience.
Um...
Thank you.

Beep!

Lights up on ZORA, FRANKLIN's *mother. She stands
smiling and lovely in the middle of the pool. There is a*
GOSPEL CHOIR *behind her.*

*Like Shirley Caesar, she speaks and the choir follows behind
her, singing.*

ZORA. Dear son...

GOSPEL CHOIR (*singing*).
        Dear son...
        I missed you today.

ZORA. I wanted to tell you

GOSPEL CHOIR.
        Wanted to tell you
        it will be ok.
        The Lord has promised that
        today is your day.

ZORA. So don't YOU worry.

GOSPEL CHOIR.
        Don't you worry
        He's already made a way.

ZORA. Your mama loves you.

GOSPEL CHOIR.
        Your mama loves you
        But don't forget to call...
        Tomorrow's not promised
        Ok... I guess that's all.

ZORA. Oh and I didn't tell you
        but I read about your show.

GOSPEL CHOIR.
        I didn't tell you
        I read bout your show

ZORA. And Lord put it on my heart

GOSPEL CHOIR.
      The Lord told me,
      Zora let's go!

ZORA. So call me soon.

GOSPEL CHOIR.
      Call me,
      and tell me where I should stay.
      Lord knows I ain't got time
      for no, AIR B AND BAYYYYY.

Scene Five

FRANKLIN *sits beside the pool sewing miniature outfits as*
MAX *and* BELLAMY *share sushi takeout.* BELLAMY *is*
wearing her own Guccis now but also has a very chic bracelet
from Tiffany's.

MAX *is wearing a Speedo.* FRANKLIN, *wearing his*
earphones, is completely immersed in his music.

Behind the sliding glass door we see members of the GOSPEL
CHOIR *moving in work tables and materials for doll*
construction. Once everything is placed they do not leave, they
watch the action silently.

BELLAMY (*to* MAX). Literally
      It was crazy,
      he just like walked over
      pulled up a chair
      and said,
      "Here's the deal.
      I don't like games
      and I don't like flakes.
      I'm a straight shooter
      and like,
      blah blah blah blah blah".

And he wasn't even hot, you know?
But he was sexy.
It was like, he had this sort of way about him
that was just, like
sexy...
And the weirdest thing was
he was dressed kind of schlubby?
Like
It was one of those things
where like I thought,
"I DEFINITELY need to take him to Barneys ASAP",
but then he picked up the menu and
he was wearing a Muller.
Just casually.
Like Vince T-shirt,
Uniqlo sweatpants
but then like
a fucking Muller
teasing me from his wrist.
It was insane.

She tosses more sushi back.

Oh my god this is so good.
(*Raising her voice.*) THANK YOU FRANKLIN!

He doesn't hear her.

MAX (*bored*). Ok...
    but get to the good part
    when did he like
    take you shopping?

BELLAMY. That's kind of the coolest thing,
    he didn't.

MAX. What?

BELLAMY. He didn't.
    It was like he knew me
    after just a few conversations
    on the site.
    After he like,
    said his whole thing.

Told me his rules or whatever
or like
"what he was looking for in a relationship"
he was like,
"oh
I have a gift for you"
and I was all like,
"wahhhhhhhhhh?"
and he was like, "duh."
And then he pulled this fucking Tiffany's bag out
and he gave me this
and like –

She gets emotional.

I honestly felt like,
this is,
you know,
like
the first time that someone,
anyone really has
like seen me?
As like
worthy?
Or something.
(*A moment. She admires her wrist.*)
I don't know.
This feels like the real thing.
I'm so happy I did it.

MAX *looks at her in disbelief.*

MAX. Bellamy?
    No.
    No no no / no no –

BELLAMY. What?

    MAX *throws a chopstick at* FRANKLIN.

MAX. This is too much,
    from both of you.
    Too much!

    FRANKLIN *looks up from his sewing, annoyed.*

FRANKLIN. What the fuck, guys?
I told you to give me thirty minutes to finish / these outfits.

MAX. I was trying to tell you
that I think
you and Bellamy
are too much.

FRANKLIN. Why are we too much?

MAX. Bellamy just told me she's in love
with a guy she met on like,
DaddyFinder.com
or some / sort of –
That's too much.

BELLAMY. That's not the site!
And I didn't say
I was / in love.

MAX. And you!
Too much!
(*He points to the movers*.)
You're fucking moving in
with your sugar daddy / after like…

FRANKLIN. Just my studio.
He's not my "sugar daddy" –
the fuck, Max?
I couldn't afford –
and
God!
He offered /
to let me have the…

BELLAMY. Geoff wrote me a letter you guys. /
It's not just some fling…

MAX. Chill out!
I'm joking
…
…
fuck.
Sensitive too.
…

　　…
　　…
　　But. You could totally have afforded it if you wanted to keep it.

FRANKLIN. No. I couldn't / have
　　even if I wanted…

　　BELLAMY *pulls out the letter. It is long, front and back for*
　　five pages, in tiny, fluid cursive.

BELLAMY. (I've never seen the handwriting
　　Of any man I've ever dated…)

MAX. Did you call your mom?

FRANKLIN. Why would I call my mom?

MAX. Because your mom could've helped you keep your
　　space.

FRANKLIN. Well
　　that's not her job.
　　Ok?
　　I figured it out without having to involve her.

　　FRANKLIN *picks back up his sewing.* BELLAMY *keeps*
　　flipping through the pages of the letter.

BELLAMY. (I can't even read this…
　　Haha…
　　Who even writes in cursive anymore)

MAX. So I guess since Mom's a no-go Daddy has to suffice?

　　FRANKLIN *sets down the sewing again.*

FRANKLIN. Dude,
　　what is your problem?
　　You don't say anything when you're lounging in the pool
　　or eating sushi on his tab
　　or any of that…
　　So I don't get what your like
　　glitch is right now.
　　Maybe no one's licking your ass tonight,
　　maybe you've lost another part?
　　I don't know,
　　and I wouldn't

because like
all you've seemed interested in talking about is my fucking
life.
…
…
…
Fuck.
Now I have a lot of shit to get done before my show next
week
so I'm going to get to it.
If you'd like to have another one of Andre's Xanaxes,
or to take another lap around Andre's pool
Or to order more sushi, ON ANDRE
the pills are over here
and towels are over there
and you can grab the iPad sitting in the kitchen.
Otherwise, please leave.
I was enjoying having your bodies here, around me, until
you started spouting your shit.

MAX *just stares at* FRANKLIN. FRANKLIN *goes back to
sewing.*

BELLAMY. You guys,
do either of you know how to read cursive?

FRANKLIN. That was just nasty.
A dick thing to say.
Fuck you.

MAX. I'm sorry.
…
(*To* BELLAMY.) Let me see the letter.

MAX *looks at the letter and tries to read it. It looks foreign.*

…
um…

FRANKLIN *looks up.*

FRANKLIN. Hand it here
…
…
fuck…

FRANKLIN *tries to decipher what's been written.*

BELLAMY. It's insane.
I, um,
I was telling Max that our date
it was
yeah
it was really beautiful.
I…
I felt like,
um,
I felt like he looked at me,
 all of me,
or was trying to,
trying to really see all of me
and like
he knew
Like
not just all the right things to say
but like all the right things I needed to hear.
The things that people don't think
I'm worth hearing
Or receiving?
And I think that's because
like
the
um
the
I guess like
the "terms of engagement"?
Were that you know
he had to prove his worth
by showing me how much he thought
I was worth,
and he thought that just meeting me
just sitting across a table from me
was worth a whole lot.
…
…
And now he's written me a letter,
and like he thinks I'm worth that
all of it,

that's next level.
Is that how Andre makes you feel Franklin?
Like he sees your worth?

FRANKLIN *looks to* BELLAMY *like he might just answer when...*

MAX. I'm actually sorry Franklin.

FRANKLIN (*passes the letter back to* BELLAMY). It doesn't matter.
I have a lot of work to get done today.

As FRANKLIN *stands to go back to work we see that the movers have stopped moving things and that* ANDRE, *for an indeterminate amount of time, has been watching the proceedings outside. He exits.*

MAX *looks back to where* ANDRE *was as though he felt something change in the air.*

MAX. (For real.)

Scene Six

ALESSIA *stands just outside the glass door, furiously taking notes on her phone in between taking quick shots of the miniature outfits* FRANKLIN *was sewing before.*

FRANKLIN *paces... trying not to look at her but failing.*

ALESSIA *looks up from her phone.*

ALESSIA. I feel like there's a lot of
    um,
    a lot of exciting things happening
    in these
    adjustments.

FRANKLIN. But...

ALESSIA. No but!
    No but at all

I just want to know where
your head is.

FRANKLIN. What does that mean?

ALESSIA. What I said.
I'm just…
I have questions.
…
…
…
These materials Franklin…

FRANKLIN. Um.
Yeah…?

ALESSIA (*looking around*). Tell me what they're meaning to
you now.
These textures are…
for lack of a better word:
richer.
This is
a bit of a departure
from the pieces I saw in your studio before.
So I just wanted to…

FRANKLIN. Right, right.
Well…
I don't know?
It like,
when,
well when Andre / invited me to like move
my studio in?
I um…

ALESSIA. Wait wait wait wait wait.
Hold on.
Andre?

ALESSIA *is on her phone typing quickly.*

FRANKLIN. Yeah, he offered / to let me –

ALESSIA *holds up her phone to* FRANKLIN.

ALESSIA. This Andre?

FRANKLIN. Yes.

ALESSIA. Oh…

   …
   …
   …
   …
   …
   …
   …
   …
   …
   …
   …
   …
   …
   …
   …
   …
   …
   …interesting.

FRANKLIN. Interesting?

ALESSIA. It's just…
   wow.
   yeah…
   So are you?

FRANKLIN. Are we what?

ALESSIA. It's none of my business
   but this,
   yeah
   it's a very generous gesture.
   So,
   anyway.
   Materials.

FRANKLIN. This has nothing to do with
   like
   the materials.
   He didn't like

he's not like buying
my materials.

ALESSIA. Honey no,
listen…
patronage is nothing
to be ashamed of
I have a trust.
Bubbe Alessia before me
escaped
Germany
dyed her hair blonde
and LITERALLY married
a Lithuanian oil magnate
so she and
all her kin could have
a patron forever.
it's fine.
It's the Medicis,
The Guggenheims,
the Rubells,
the Gettys,
that are responsible for all the art we love.
So don't be ashamed.

FRANKLIN. Yeah but…
he's not.
It's not like / a Medici thing.

ALESSIA. Can you –
I don't want this to feel
Like I'm
like the Gestapo or something.
I'm just trying to connect…
trying to make sense of it all
because
what we're doing.
What we're undertaking.
Is not just about me putting your art
On display
For a bunch of like
Rich people to gawk at…

it's
a relationship.

FRANKLIN. Yeah, totally.
Um, materials
the um… well I'm / using a lot.

ALESSIA. God kill me
(I sound like a
Manson Girl,
or like
Bonnie Nettles or something…)
But
Franklin I'm serious.
I want to make a major change
to the gallery
to what we do
what we're known for and
since…
truly,
truly
since encountering your work I've known
that you could be that change
for the gallery
and the gallery could be a landscape
of change
for you and your relationship
to the entire art world.

FRANKLIN. Right,
totally I agree.
I know. I feel the same.

ALESSIA. So you have to let me in.
I was just asking some questions.
I was just trying to make sense of the work
as it is now
because it's different.
Significantly so.
There's silk in some of these,
wool. You didn't.
You weren't as considered

with your dolls' sartorial expressions
before.
They're on display now.
I'm trying to understand what that means for / the work.

FRANKLIN. I want to call the show "Daddy".
A spoken one
with quotes.
…
…
…
Like the dolls are speaking for themselves?
The materials.
The reason I've
changed them
the reason
they've become more expressive
is because…
you…
when…
When you're in the presence of Daddy
he demands that you be presentable.
That you stand up straight
that you dress smart.
Daddy bought you that nice shirt why aren't you wearing it?
This is –
an important conceit of the show
as I see it now.
If these dolls
are possibly me.
I want each of the daddies in the room
to see me.
Dressed smart.
Standing at attention.
Just like daddies always like.
…
…
…

There's a pause.

ALESSIA *slowly begins to smile.*

ALESSIA. That's
    so
    demented.
    So deliciously demented.
    I love.
    This…
    Yes. I love.
    It's very clear,
    these ideas.
    There was a muddiness before
    that I wasn't seeing,
    I think that's what I'll have to say to some of the collectors
    who came to the previews.
    That there's a rapid maturation happening right now
    for you.
    Your craft is tightening
    so the work is shifting. Yes.
    I'm going to go have my assistant
    type this up for us.
    Get on a new press release…
    But yes.
    That's all I wanted.
    I knew.
    You're the change.
    This is significant. Truly.

ALESSIA *grabs her things and exits after quickly kissing him.*

FRANKLIN *looks back to where she exited to see the*
GOSPEL CHOIR. *Standing before him.*

GOSPEL CHOIR (*slowly singing*).
    Dadddddddyyyyyyy
    Dadddddddddyyyyyyy
    Dadddddddddyyyyy
    Daddy won't nothing but a
    "shhhhhhh"
    Daddy won't nothing but a
    "shhhhhhh"
    Daddy won't nothing but a
    "shhhhhhh"

FRANKLIN *begins to shiver.*

Scene Seven

ANDRE *and* FRANKLIN *sit upstage on one of the chaise lounges, deep in conversation.* ANDRE *is drinking a negroni, slowly, trying to listen.*

The GOSPEL CHOIR *is there. They are sitting around the pool watching the action of the scene play out, perhaps commenting with light gestures.*

ANDRE. So you don't like her?

FRANKLIN. No.
    I love her.
    She's –
    I LOVE her.
    It's just that I do think that I see the work differently than you do.

ANDRE. That's not fair.

FRANKLIN. Yes it is.
    It completely is,
    it hits me, like
    my eyes see with the same angers and fears and joys and frustrations as hers.

ANDRE. And mine can't?
    Beauty is beauty is beauty, Franklin.
    No matter whose eyes are seeing it.
    I saw the show,
    all the sugar,
    shaped like that?
    Built that high?
    How could I not –
    How could I not cry at the sheer beauty of it?
    Of her / immensity? Her –

FRANKLIN. That's my problem with her!
    That's what I don't like.
    It –
    Like…
    For you, y'know?

You get to miss her subtlety.
You get to fly by her pain and bathe in her spectacle.
You get to forget the little black boys melting in the summer
sun.
You get to be there, in her nightmare,
her dream,
and it's not a nightmare
or a dream
you're sharing it's a nightmare
or a dream
you're witnessing.
But I share it
some part of it
even if my dreams don't look like hers
because
they feel like hers.
And I know yours don't
or can't because
I don't feel joy about her beauty
I feel an orgy of feeling
that slides from elation
to pain to wonder
to pain to anger
to pain…
to unknown
unnamed spaces of feeling
so that often I don't know how to feel
when I leave
only that I felt
and felt everything
and "everything" feels more valuable
than gold.
A sort of alchemy
where the primary ingredient is her pain.
Which is a specific pain
a female pain
a black pain
an inherited pain
a rejected pain.
A litany.
And your ability

to ignore that pain
in order
to just see beauty…
as simply beautiful.
That's my problem.
That's what scares me about what I do.
Why I do.
Why she frustrates me so much
because alchemy comes at a cost
and if I've seen that you've missed her everything
then she must have too;
and what does that cost her?
What is it going to cost me?

ANDRE *takes a moment and tries to listen. He lights a cigarette.*

ANDRE.…
   …
   …
   …
   …
I think –
I think I can start to see how
well,
no
because…
I guess for me art was always only supposed to be
impressive.
Beautiful.
That's how it was framed for me
when I showed an interest
when it started to excite me.
I'm from the school of aesthetics.
That's how I was taught to value work
and understand it
from a place that asked me to answer
what its beauty meant to me
and how what it meant to me
might intersect with what
it meant to the canon.
   …

...
...
When I got my first piece
my father gave it to me,
it was a Degas.
A study:
two boys in a field
running after a beast
(probably a dog)
that you could barely make out through the scratches.
Sort of a trifle,
but a Degas
and special
because of the boy in the foreground.
It was beautiful.
Overflowing with beauty in the simplest way.
He was the most fully formed object in the image
a square jaw beneath black hair
and offset eyes.
I couldn't stop staring at him
as my father placed the piece in my hands and
told me to make sure I put it somewhere it could be seen.
So I did.
Because that's how he understood art:
as a thing
you frame and hang to be seen
and I think
that
you know the only
thing
artistic I inherited from him
was that...
a quality that you
called "gauche"
Not too long ago
...
...
...
...
I must have felt something
something close to that everything

you felt but
I don't know if I felt it with the depth
you've just articulated, and
I'm not sure why
that could be.
If perhaps an appreciation of beauty
blocks you from that or…
But I want to learn.
I think I just see beauty in pain?

FRANKLIN *gets a text. He looks at his phone.*

And I think,
I mean,
especially now since / you've arrived – …

FRANKLIN. Oh my god…
Fuck.

ANDRE. What?

FRANKLIN. I…
Wow. It was, um,
Alessia…
"The collectors are over the moon with the new direction."
she says.
Oh my god, this is –
but I'm –
sorry
since I've gotten here?

ANDRE (*embracing him*). No.
No.
No.
This night is about you now.
You are so fucking special.
Worried for nothing!

FRANKLIN. No, / shut up.

ANDRE. And…
well,
I didn't want to tell you but
Gregory was impressed too.

FRANKLIN. What?

ANDRE. My friend.
 Gregory from Frieze?
 He's been wanting to write about my collection for a while
 now
 and when he came by I took him through your studio
 and he was very excited about this
 phenomenal artist who'd perched in my makeshift
 live/work in the hills.

 FRANKLIN *looks over and smiles… attempting to hide his discomfort.*

FRANKLIN. Oh.

ANDRE. Yeah, there's going to be a small feature done on the
 website
 then,
 he's going to follow me around your show.
 Isn't that exciting?

FRANKLIN. Um…
 Yeah.

ANDRE. I think it's important.

 FRANKLIN *gets up and walks to the other side of the room.*

FRANKLIN. Totally.

ANDRE. Because it's like I was saying
 since you've come into my life
 I've…
 I want to be supportive of you,
 the artist.
 I don't want you to ever think,
 ever,
 that you're anything less to me than
 the immensely fascinating man that I think you are.

 He embraces FRANKLIN.

 Even if you're still my little Naomi
 when the lights are off.

 FRANKLIN *looks up, serious now.*

FRANKLIN. Is he putting that in the feature?

ANDRE. What?

Pause.

FRANKLIN *attempts to find his words carefully.*

FRANKLIN. Is he putting that in the feature?
That I'm
I'm your "Little Naomi"?
I –
…
…
You know that
…
Like
…
Alessia was really into what I showed her.
Like really into it.
But she was like,
"Oh – "
with a really long pause
when I mentioned who owned the house where my new
"studio" was located.
"Oh – " with a
like
a really long pause.
Like,
a raised eyebrow.
"Oh – "
…
…
…
And I didn't care because I
I like
I like you, you know?
I think you're dope.
You like… I don't know,
That night you looked at me
that first night
after the club
and it was like

it was like
there was music playing
and
and
you
and me
were standing on the middle of a stage
lights burning down on us
beading our skin with sweat
and the whole world could see us
and they couldn't take their eyes off us
and I was like,
I was into that.
And
then everything started moving really fast
and I was into that too
but...
I don't know.
I don't know that I want the actual whole world
to be staring up at me.
I don't know that I want to like,
be on a stage.
You know?
I don't want to be the guy who gets an
"Oh – "
with a really long pause after every introduction of my
boyfriend.
...
...
Are you?
Are you even my boyfriend?

FRANKLIN *sits down. He puts his face in between his hands.*

Like,
Alessia really liked my work,
what I'm doing.
She's –
She's saying she is going to be putting all this push behind
the show
and like,

that's a lot of pressure.
It's great but it's like,
…
do you get what I'm saying Andre?
Like,
Why would you – ?

ANDRE *finishes smoking his cigarette and puts it out. He
has the last sip of his negroni.*

ANDRE. Franklin stand up.

FRANKLIN *looks up at him, confused.*

I said,
Stand up.

FRANKLIN. Andre…
are you going to listen
to what I have to say
or / are you just –

ANDRE *throws the negroni glass against the wall. The*
GOSPEL CHOIR *reacts.*

ANDRE. STAND UP!

FRANKLIN *does.*

All I do is listen!
I don't stop listening,
I listen in places deeper than you think you can penetrate!
…
…
…
Come over here.

FRANKLIN *begins to slowly walk over.* ANDRE *reaches
out and grabs* FRANKLIN. *It should be a bit frightening, a
surprising display of raw virility.*

(*Hugging him.*) I'm sorry…

ANDRE *begins to move with him, an awkward beginning to
a slow dance. As they sway back and forth* FRANKLIN*'s feet
slowly move atop* ANDRE*'s, their dance growing more fluid
and impressive with each passing line.*

Honestly.
I'm sorry.
I just –
I want the best for you Franklin. You're special. /
…

FRANKLIN. You don't have /
to just say

ANDRE. NO.
That first night
After the club,
For me, it was

…
it was, as if,
when I looked at you I saw this person who I wanted to want
me.
Immediately.
I wanted you to see me as
a sort of –
a figure you could depend on?
Because I immediately became your dependant,
when you started deconstructing my entire –
my life's worth essentially,
I then knew I needed you.
And more than that I needed you to need me.

…
…

*The opening notes to "Father Figure" begin to play again,
but this time* FRANKLIN *doesn't notice. Instead*
FRANKLIN *looks up at* ANDRE *as they glide around the
edge of the pool like Rogers and Astaire.*

Am I your boyfriend Franklin?
No.
No I'm not.
I think that's been clear since we met.
I don't want to be your boyfriend
or anyone else's.
What does that even look like?
(A man my age.)

…

…
A boyfriend?
No. I…
I want to take care of you.
I think you made it perfectly clear that night who –
Franklin,
I want you to know you don't have to pretend to be strong
with me.

Gracefully, ANDRE *disentangles himself from the dance and
makes his way to the* GOSPEL CHOIR *who have started to
assemble upstage near the glass sliding door.*

ANDRE *begins to sing 'Father Figure' by George Michael
(at the time of printing we only had the rights to the song in
production not in print… so Google the lyrics and KNOW it
looked good on the page).*

As ANDRE *sings, the* GOSPEL CHOIR *follows behind.*
ANDRE *sings earnestly, but this doesn't mean he sings well.*

FRANKLIN *continues to dance as though with a partner,
oblivious until the moment he isn't that* ANDRE *is singing a
pop song to an audience.*

The more he sings the more emboldened ANDRE *becomes.
Perhaps he dances, maybe he begins to disrobe, kicking off
his shoes.* FRANKLIN *continues to dance alone as though
upon the feet of another but as he does so we see tears start
to form in the corner of his eyes.*

ANDRE *is now in the pool, the* GOSPEL CHOIR *behind
him in full-tilt revelry.*

FRANKLIN, *overcome by some welling grief or sadness,
collapses out of the dance and onto the ground.*

FRANKLIN (*to some invisible*   GOSPEL CHOIR.
ANDRE). I'm fine.   I will be your father
I just, like…
need a few moments.
Ok?
…
…
Ok?

ANDRE.
I will be your

GOSPEL CHOIR.
I will be your preacher

ANDRE.
Father

GOSPEL CHOIR.
I will be your father

ANDRE.
I'll be your daddy

GOSPEL CHOIR.
I will be the one who loves you

ANDRE.
Till the end of time

FRANKLIN *looks up and once again sees past his current reality and into this other one where* ANDRE *is halfway through a George Michael song with a choir.*

FRANKLIN *shakes and shivers and, with a new burst of energy, opens up a dam of tears and wails. Once again, back in his reality.*

BLACKOUT.

In the darkness we hear the sounds of sniffles as FRANKLIN *sniffs back his tears and the sounds of bodies moving through water as the* GOSPEL CHOIR *and* ANDRE *move out of the pool.*

Then we hear the sound of a phone ringing. Loud and distinct: RING RING RING.

It should echo around the theatre listlessly until finally we hear:

BEEP!

FRANKLIN (*voice-over*). Hi, you've reached Franklin.
Sorry I uh,
I can't get to the phone right now.
But if you need anything just leave a message

Or, like, send me an email
or a text
and I'll get back to you at my earliest convenience.
Um…
Thank you.

BEEP!

A pinhole of light illuminates just ZORA*'s face.* GOSPEL
CHOIR *hums a score to the following. It, once again, should
feel almost like a Shirley Caesar song.*

ZORA. Son
you've being laying heavy on my heart
these past few weeks.
…
…
I don't know exactly where you've been
or who
you been running with
but it's left my spirit in a deep unease.
…
…
This morning
I got on my knees
and I prayed for you.
…
…
And let me tell ya
what the Lord's gonna do.
…
…
He's gonna ease your pain
at least that's what he said
He said don't you worry,
this all part of his plan…
…
…
He said I shouldn't have to tell you
You would already know.
If you weren't too busy
rippin' and runnin' up and down the road.

...
...
I'm calling for the last time
before I show up next week.
Don't let me find out
you ain't been prayin' constantly.

...

...
This show is important
or so you seemed to say
so make it a priority and get on your knees and pray.

...

...
Like Solomon says in Proverbs
chapter ten, verse one
a foolish son is a grief to his mother.
Don't be a grief baby.

...

...
I love you son,
I guess that is all.
OH!
Since you never asked,
I found my own hotel. (It's somewhere real expensive,
it's called the SOFITEL!)

End of Act One.

ACT TWO (FRANKLIN + ZORA)

Scene One

In darkness the sound of cannonballs and revelry cascade from the stage and ricochet throughout the space.

As the lights rise we see ZORA *standing among the aftermath of a wild pool party. Neon lights fluoresce from the pool and* ZORA *stands there illuminated, dressed in her outfit for the opening: a nice but not necessarily chic pantsuit (although given the way she holds herself, the outfit feels more expensive than it is), her handbag in the crook of her arm.*

FRANKLIN *makes his way outside to her with two drinks in his hands. He hands her the rosé and smiles shyly before taking a sip of his drink.*

A few members of the GOSPEL CHOIR, *stragglers from the party, can be seen wandering in the back behind the glass door with little black dolls in their hands.*

ZORA *looks at him for a moment before speaking.*

ZORA. Congratulations son.

FRANKLIN (*nervous*). Mom
    this was
    it's…

ZORA. So this how you living now?

FRANKLIN (*cowering*). No, Mama
    it's –
    like
    it's not like that.
    Andre just said I could have the after-party / here so…

ZORA. Don't be ashamed baby.
    It's nice.
    Real nice.
    Just a shame all of this been keeping you from answering your phone.

(*Pause, a raise of the eyebrow.*)
Who knows though…
Maybe the calls weren't going through.
I'm sure up here they pay to keep the signal weak.
Seclusion.
They like that…

ZORA *takes a liberal sip of her drink.*

FRANKLIN. Mama
    I told you,
    I just,
    I got busy.
    The show…
    and like…
    I don't know.
    It's like –
    (*Like a teenager.*) Ughhhhhhhhhh.

ZORA *looks at him. She sees through his lie but why argue?*
She's more interested in that "ughhhhh".

ZORA. Yeah that show,
    it was something.

FRANKLIN. Mama…

ZORA. What?
    I'm serious.
    It was something.
    If I had known white people were gonna love those little
    dolls you were always making I would've had you out there
    selling them when you were little.
    Joe Jackson style.
    Then maybe I wouldn't have broke my back sending you to
    that damn art school
    You could've sent yourself.

FRANKLIN *rolls his eyes and finishes his drink.*

FRANKLIN. You want another?

ZORA. Don't think I'm not proud baby.
    I am.
    I mean…
    You –

You made a room full of white folk walk around with little
coon babies on their arms like they were Madonna or
something.
Ha!
Angelina Jolie.
It was a sight to behold.
Coon babies…
They loved it.

FRANKLIN. Mama, don't / call

ZORA. That's what they are!
Coon babies.
That what they used to call them when I was growing up
right there in the stores.
"COON BABIES".
We used to think they were ugly.
Nobody wanted to get them.
You'd just see coon baby
after coon baby
after coon baby lining the aisle at Christmas time.
That's whatcha should of called the show:
"Coon Babies".
Better yet: "Coon Babies at Christmas Time".
Everybody likes Christmas.
I don't know what you were doing calling it "Daddy".
What's that all about?

*ZORA looks at him harder this time as though she's willing
a truth out of him that she knows he won't give.*

FRANKLIN. It's about a lot of things
that
like
are personal?
And like,
I don't know.
Alessia thought /
that

Just as he says her name ALESSIA *and* ANDRE *enter
through the sliding doors.*

ANDRE. AND THE LAST OF YOUR ADMIRERS HAVE
    TURNED IN FOR THE NIGHT!
    (*To* ZORA.) Exciting, wasn't it?

    ZORA *nods*. ANDRE *looks at her, a bit nervous in her
    presence*.

    ALESSIA *excitedly rushes over and hugs* FRANKLIN.

ALESSIA. Franklin,
    that was everything and more than I expected.
    That –
    Franklin it was perfect.
    Sold out.
    Completely.
    Your first show.
    (*To* ZORA.) You should be very proud of your son.
    That was…
    That's –
    It's VERY RARE for an artist of your son's –
    well he's just so fresh, you know?
    You don't see a green artist do this well on their first show.

ZORA. Well he's blessed.
    Been that way his whole life.
    The Lord has a lot in store for him.

FRANKLIN. Mama…

    ALESSIA *shifts uncomfortably*.

ALESSIA. Yeah…
    Well I'm sure a lot of people
    on all planes of consciousness
    are going to have a lot in store for Franklin.
    (*Turns back to* FRANKLIN.)
    My father,
    back when he ran the gallery
    he used to wax poetic
    about the eighties
    this moment
    when people actually CARED
    about the work
    about art.

And showed how much they cared
by putting their money where their mouth is
but like
that culture
sort of died.
And it took a lot of great
great work with it.
Because if no one is getting paid,
you know?
If no one's getting paid then no one is making the work
and I remember
my father
he told me
as I was taking over...
he said,
"Alessia good luck
you've chosen to build a life
in a mortuary
you're among the dead
when you work in the art world now
you won't ever see it living
the way I did."
And that haunted me.
But
(*She begins to get emotional.*)
Today I think I saw it alive
I saw the start of something.
Of some sort of liveness
a resurrection.
And your son is responsible for that!
Your son.

FRANKLIN....

   ...

ALESSIA. Ok...
I think it's my bedtime.
But, more tomorrow.
This –
You should be very proud.
This is a true accomplishment.
Bathe in it.

She hugs FRANKLIN *again and then with a wave* ALESSIA *exits.*

ANDRE *looks over to* FRANKLIN *nervously as* ZORA *finishes her wine and sets down her glass.*

ANDRE. Zora,
    let me show you your, uh
    your room.
    It's all set / up and

ZORA. That's ok, Andre. I'm very comfortable at my hotel.
    (*She pulls out her phone.*)
    I'm just going to –
    (If I can figure this damn Uber thing out)
    I'm just gonna head on over there.
    it was a very nice party / you threw for…

FRANKLIN. Andre,
    Mama's fine,
    I'll get her an Uber.

FRANKLIN *pulls out his phone.*

ANDRE. Zora,
    honestly
    you would offend me if you didn't stay.
    A mother shouldn't visit her son and be locked away from
    him in a hotel.
    (That's –
    no.
    I won't have it.)
    You're staying here.
    I'll be right back,
    I'm just going to make sure everything in the room is perfect.

ANDRE *exits.* ZORA *looks over at her son.*

ZORA. (So this how you living now…)

FRANKLIN *looks away.* ZORA *walks over and grabs his face tenderly. She places her temple against his.*

(*Whispering.*) I love you baby, you know that, right?

FRANKLIN *nods his head slowly.*

FRANKLIN. Yes Mama.
   I love you too.

ZORA (*playfully*). No you don't.

FRANKLIN. I love you times a million.

ZORA (*she looks at him deeply*). I love you times infinity,
   and you know I won't ever steer you wrong.

   FRANKLIN *doesn't move.*

   Something ain't right
   I don't know if it's him or this place
   or what
   but right now…?
   My spirit is unsettled.
   …
   …
   You been praying?

FRANKLIN. Why?

ZORA. Because I don't think the Lord would've led you here.

FRANKLIN. Mama…

ZORA. Listen to me…
   When I walked in here
   the Lord laid some scripture on my spirit.

   FRANKLIN *moves away from* ZORA *but she grabs his arm
   and pulls him close, staring at him.*

   When I walked into that gallery you looked at me with fear
   and for a moment your eyes glazed over like you hated me.
   You can't hide that from me.
   I see you.
   I see you baby
   and that –
   in that moment
   that won't a look from my Franklin.
   I don't know who looked at me but that look's been haunting
   me all night.
   And when I walked in here all I heard was Second Timothy
   Chapter three: "But know this, / that in the last days

FRANKLIN. Mama stop.

ZORA. Perilous times will come. For men will be lovers of themselves, lovers of money, boasters, proud, blasphemers, disobedient to parents, / unthankful, unholy.

FRANKLIN *starts fidgeting now, uncomfortable in his body like an adolescent.*

FRANKLIN (*whining*). Mama stoooooopppppppp.

ZORA *notices this and worry flashes deeply across her face but she keeps going:*

ZORA. Unloving, unforgiving slanderers, without self-control, brutal, despisers of good. Traitors, headstrong, haughty lovers of pleasure rather than lovers of God. Having a form of / godliness but denying its power

FRANKLIN *puts his hands up to his ears and begins stomping his feet on the ground.*

FRANKLIN (*still whining in his voice*). You don't know anything about him, Mama. Calm this dowwwwnnnnn.

ZORA *recognizes this but has no idea why it is appearing again now. She does what she used to do with these situations: ignore it.*

ZORA. And from such people turn away! For of this sort are those who creep into households and make captives of the gullible. Loaded down with sins, led away by various lusts. Always / learning

ANDRE *re-enters and* FRANKLIN *immediately runs to him and grabs him at the torso, throwing his head onto* ANDRE's *chest.*

FRANKLIN (*whining*). SHE WON'T STOPPPPPPP-AH.

ANDRE *looks at* FRANKLIN *for a second as though wondering if he should follow his impulse to place a hand on his head.*

ZORA. Franklin?
Something's got a hold of you.
And I don't like it.

ZORA *looks at* ANDRE. ANDRE *places a hand on* FRANKLIN's *head.*

Scene Two

The lights rise on ANDRE *and* ZORA *sitting across from each other at a table just upstage of the pool. Salmon, eggs, bagels, and orange juice are strewn out before them.*

A third plate sits between them completely clean and untouched.

They eat in silence. ANDRE *is reading the news from his phone as* ZORA *picks at her food, unimpressed. The* GOSPEL CHOIR *looks on and we feel* FRANKLIN*'s ears on them.*

ZORA. Is there any, um…
    is there any salt?
    Or um
    or pepper?

ANDRE (*looking up*). What was that?

ZORA. Is there any salt here?
    Or pepper?

ANDRE. Oh!
    Um, yes.
    Yes there is but…
    It should be seasoned to –
    I'll go,
    just give me one moment.

    ANDRE *exits.*

    ZORA *takes a bite and looks at the pool and the sky and city down below the hill.*

    ANDRE *returns with three large grinders.*

    I didn't know if you'd prefer pink Himalayan
    or just natural sea salt so I brought both.
    And here's the pepper.

    ZORA *laughs.*

ZORA. That's a lot of contraption for just a little salt and
    pepper.

ANDRE. What?

ZORA. I said that's a lot of contraption.

ANDRE. Oh.

ZORA. I don't even know –
    What's "pink Himalayan"?

ANDRE. Oh!
    It's um…
    well it's a sort of
    (*He laughs*.)
    Well it's healthy?
    Healthier,
    I guess than…
    than…

ZORA. Than salt for normal folk.

ANDRE. No no no no no
    I just / mean –

ZORA. I'll try some of that pink stuff.

    ANDRE *hands her the salt and she begins to apply it
    liberally to her breakfast, before picking up the pepper and
    doing the same.*

    GRIND

    GRIND

    GRIND

    GRIND

    GRIND

    When is Franklin getting up?
    He said he wanted to take me to
    Lacam or something
    but if he don't get up
    I'm gonna take my behind on down to that Rose Bowl
    he used to talk about so much.

ANDRE. Oh the Rose Bowl
    is a delight,
    but you really should let him take you to LACMA.
    You should see it before he ends up there.

ZORA. Oh!
You think he's gonna get in a museum?

ANDRE. Of course.
Don't you?

ZORA. I'm his mother.
I think he'll get into LACMA, BACMA, FAFSA
wherever the hell he wanna be
when he wanna be there.
I'm asking bout you.
What makes YOU so sure.
(*She laughs.*)

ANDRE. Because he's a true artist.
A true talent.
It's undeniable.

ZORA. It's undeniable?
I like that.
undeniable.
huh!
....
...
...
What do you do Andre?

ANDRE *looks at* ZORA. *A sentence swallowed back down.*

ANDRE. I'm a collector.

ZORA. That's a job?

ANDRE. In a sense, yes.

ZORA. If buying things for my home could be a job
I'd put Queen Elizabeth to shame.
That's a real nice life.

ANDRE. It can be.

ZORA. And what do your people do?

ANDRE. Which people?

ZORA. Oh excuse me,
I mean your parents,

family.
What're their professions?
Is collecting the family business?

ANDRE. Oh no, art was my proclivity.
It was never really...
but the family,
they do all sorts of things.
None of it of much interest.
Or with much interest.

...
...
...
What about you Zora?
What does your family do?
What do you do?

ZORA. Franklin's never talked about that?

ANDRE. He doesn't talk of home much.

ZORA. Hmmm...
you ever ask?

ANDRE. I –

ZORA. We come from a factory town.
Furniture folk.
Lot of work with our hands.
Before that
we were tobacco folk.
Again.
Work with our hands.
Even all the way out here
Where they got different kind of salts (pink AND white)
Franklin still found a way to keep working with those hands.

ANDRE *starts to feel the conversation turning.*

ANDRE. I should go see if he's up.

ZORA. Andre?

ANDRE. Yes, Zora?

ZORA. What are you?
What is this?

ANDRE. What do you mean?

ZORA. You know what I mean.
　　I'm not trying to be rude
　　or anything like that.
　　Let's just,
　　speak on what this is.

This is the turn he anticipated.

The GOSPEL CHOIR, *looking on, put their hands over their mouths, holding in their breath.*

ANDRE. Well

　　…
　　…

ZORA. Well?
　　Are you his mentor…
　　a schoolteacher…
　　are you his friend…
　　his lover?

ANDRE. I think this is a conversation for you and Franklin.
　　And moreover,
　　it feels like crass early morning conversation.
　　I feel like the relationship between Franklin and I
　　is pretty evident.
　　I know you've not been here very long
　　but I feel as though I have a shit face for poker
　　so…
　　it is exactly as it seems to you.

ZORA. Which is?

ANDRE. Which is as it seems.

ZORA. Ha!

ANDRE. You seem incredulous Zora.

ZORA. Well –

ANDRE. Incredulous means to / be

ZORA. I know what the word means!

The GOSPEL CHOIR *lets their hands down and begin to breathe again.*

FRANKLIN. Mama?

FRANKLIN *has entered.*

ZORA. Franklin!
How long were you there?

FRANKLIN. What do you mean?

ANDRE *walks over to* FRANKLIN *and kisses him tenderly.*

ANDRE. I think you and your mother should head to LACMA she has questions about our relationship.

FRANKLIN. Questions?

ANDRE. Zora,
you were a wonderful breakfast companion.
I apologize if my
zeal
or
embarrassment
got in the way of us having a real conversation.

FRANKLIN. A real conversation about what?

ANDRE. I'm going to go …
have fun with your mother.

ANDRE *exits.*

FRANKLIN. A real conversation about what?

ZORA. What's y'all's relationship?
That your boyfriend?

FRANKLIN....

…

…

We are definitely partners.
I don't know that I'd call us boyfriends.

ZORA. What would you call yourselves?

The GOSPEL CHOIR *stand.*

GOSPEL CHOIR.
>I will be…
>I will be…
>I will be…
>I will be…

FRANKLIN….
>…
>…
>…
>…
>…
>…Bonded.

Scene Three

Behind the closed sliding glass door FRANKLIN *is working studiously on a new soft sculpture with the* GOSPEL CHOIR. *We can see from where we are that whatever they are working on is much larger than the pieces we saw before. Perhaps he is working on a foot that's quite large or an arm he could wrap around his body.*

Outside, MAX *and* BELLAMY *are sitting on chaise lounges.* BELLAMY *is reading to* MAX *from her iPhone with the precision of someone who's not used to hearing gangly words crawl from her mouth.*

BELLAMY. "While holding these crude, misshapen dolls one feels like a priest of the Vodun, or some other mystic. Touched by a spirit that's frightening in its purity."
>…
>uh it's so long…
>But ok,
>I get the point.
>They liked it?
>or something…

MAX *grabs the phone from her and scrolls down.*

MAX. Yes!
    But –
    ugh...
    l wanted to read you this:
    "Moreover the young artist,
    besides capturing the imaginations of Beverly Hills' young
    and hip,
    if vapid,
    contemporary / art crowd..."

BELLAMY. That's us right?

MAX. "he ALSO seems to have cast a spell on
    a certain prodigious collector
    who invited the artist and his virile cohorts back to his
    expansive Bel Air estate to celebrate
    into the wee hours of the night after his opening."

    MAX *looks at* BELLAMY *expectantly.*

BELLAMY. That's
    amazing.
    Oh my god!
    Can you send me that?
    I NEED
    to Insta that quote.
    Like, /
    that's major.

MAX. No but
    like
    you're not getting it.
    Like,
    what the fuck?

BELLAMY. I don't get what you're saying.

MAX. I'm saying
    WHAT
    THE
    FUCK.
    That's sketch man...
    like super super sketch.

BELLAMY *takes her phone back from* MAX *and puts it in her purse. Behind them* ZORA *has walked into the work space and is watching* FRANKLIN *work. She has a towel in her hand.* (*Maybe she says something to him we can't hear every now and then.*)

BELLAMY. Why is that sketch Max?

MAX. The fact that
    this "critic"
    like…
    (*He whispers.*)
    mentioned Andre?
    I mean…
    SKETCH.
    Which just
    I mean…
    that's not ok?
    Not.
    Ok.
    Right?
    …
    …
    (*Back to normal voice.*)
    Because
    like
    Ethics in Journalism
    you know?
    Or whatever.

BELLAMY. Max they didn't say his name.
    You're being so extra right now.

MAX. No Bellamy.
    No…
    This is fucked up.
    A review would've been:
    "Went to Franklin's show
    it was great
    there were dolls
    that looked like Franklin
    wearing little suits
    and shoes.

It was pretty creepy.
Voodoo references?
Cabbage Patch Kids?
Tamagotchis!
Etc.
Go see it."
…
…
See,
Easy
ethical journalism:
Focus on the work.
You know?
Making it…
or even like putting that into the minds
of your readers is just like
irresponsible.
You know?
That's like that time that
like
that director?
You remember?
He was like "it's yours
just
all you have to do
is like
just…"
and then
he like
invited me on his plane?
To go with him and the producer to Coachella
and he was like
…
(*He does something with his hands.*)
and like
the "just"
was like
obviously
for me
him
and the producer

to like…
fuck
or whatever.
Mile High Club.
And because people saw us together
all weekend
and there was that dumb picture of us
in a golf cart together
on WeHo Confidential
everybody started saying we were fucking
after I got cast in his pilot
And like
that was gross.
you know?

BELLAMY. No I don't know Max
because you did fuck him.
And you did get the part
because you fucked him.

MAX *looks at* BELLAMY *like she's stupid.*

MAX. Yeah
and I regretted it Bellamy.
I only did it because
I was horny.
And he was there, not to get a part.
Because
ew
And he wanted me to date him.
Like
I could have dated him
and then I would have been the like
fucking LEAD
in a movie that premiered at Telluride.
But I didn't
because
like
I don't know…

ZORA *slides open the door quietly and walks outside.*
BELLAMY *and* MAX *don't notice.*

BELLAMY. You're being super weird
      Max
      and you're like projecting…

MAX. Projecting or protecting?
      Because / I –

ZORA. What're y'all talking about?

MAX looks up, surprised.

MAX. Oh, I'm sorry Ms Zora.

ZORA. Why are you sorry.

BELLAMY. Because…

There's a pause.

ZORA. Because y'all were talking about my son laying up in
      bed with Methuselah?
      HaHa.

MAX laughs.

BELLAMY. Methuselah?

ZORA hugs BELLAMY and looks over at MAX, smiling.

ZORA. Aw baby… I'm just playing.
      What do you all think of Grandpa though?
      Mr Andre?

*She pulls a chair up and sits with them. Crossing her legs
and immediately holding court.*

BELLAMY. We really weren't talking about
      that Miss Zora
      we were actually talking about
      some of Max's career decisions.

ZORA looks past BELLAMY to MAX.

ZORA. Oh you were?

MAX (*quietly*). Yes ma'am.

ZORA. Hmmm…
      Tell me more bout this projecting

and protecting.
What was all that about.

BELLAMY *and* MAX *look at each other.*

MAX....
    Well / I –

BELLAMY. Max was just telling a story
    about
    a man who had taken advantage of him.
    When he was first starting out.
    And he was just saying that
    like,
    he's scared
    of how things about Franklin's living situation
    might be viewed,
    and I said I thought he was projecting.

ZORA *looks at* BELLAMY *for a moment before turning her attention to* MAX.

ZORA. Well Max, you do always seem
    to know what's going on.
    You really think Andre is
    taking advantage of Franklin?

MAX. Um...

    MAX *looks to* BELLAMY.

    It's like...
    it's one of those things
    where I don't really know
    how to answer that
    because nothing gives me any reason
    to think that.
    So I guess no.
    I just, sometimes I worry about Franklin
    and I /
    know...

ZORA. You should worry bout him
    you both should.
    Y'all been glued at the hip since he got here.
    That's what good friends are for

they should be the ones who can look you in the face
and tell you they worried.

BELLAMY. I'm not worried Ms Zora.
    I –
    Andre's so fun, he's a lot like Franklin.

ZORA. Well I haven't seen the fun yet...

MAX. Ditto!

    She looks at MAX *for a moment.*

ZORA. Max!
    Why haven't you and Franklin ever...?

    BELLAMY *starts to laugh.*

    That's none of my business.
    It's just...
    Methuselah!
    I'll tell you right now I don't like him.
    I don't trust him.
    There's something creepy about him.
    He –
    I don't know.
    I can't put my finger right on it. He just.
    He reminds me...
    He's REAL similar to Franklin's father.

MAX. Really?
    Franklin's never told us anything about his dad.

BELLAMY. That's true.
    It's kind of weird.

ZORA. It ain't weird.
    He just don't know him.
    I was...
    Well
    in my younger days
    I would rip and run
    up and down the streets
    and you know I met this –
    He was a real man.
    Strong.

He'd pick me up
with one hand
that kind of strong.
And he took care of me.
He was my –
he was at the time,
the love of my life.
After,
you know
it was Franklin. But,
at that time…
he was my world.
Couldn't close my eyes without feeling his on me
couldn't speak without hoping the words would live inside of
his ears when they left my mouth.
I would've torn my insides out if he asked me to…
Or so I thought.
'Cause then,
you know I got pregnant
and
all of a sudden
this little idea on my insides
was all I could see.
My eyelids were branded with an image I could almost make
out every time I closed my eyes,
when I spoke the words danced outta my mouth and right
down to my belly before they could get any further.
He didn't like that
and suddenly,
he didn't feel the need to be strong no more
if he couldn't be strong just for me.
I don't think he ever was.
He wore the strength like his mask.
He was worried this idea would see under it
see his weakness.
And I think this
you know
Andre?
I think he's the same
Except his mask is made of money.
Fraid of an idea he don't even know he's conceived.

But who knows,
I've been made a fool by better men.

BELLAMY *and* MAX *sit in silence with* ZORA.

After a while:

BELLAMY. I'm sorry that happened to you Ms Zora.

MAX.... Yeah that was –
wow.

ZORA. There ain't nothing to be sorry about
that test is behind me.
A long time ago my Lord (Father God!)
whispered in my ear "You passed
now let it go. And give it a good Go'On."

ZORA *looks at* BELLAMY, *smiles, then stands. She turns her back to* BELLAMY, *revealing the zipper on the back of her dress.*

Unzip this for me baby.

She does.

You know I haven't been in a pool in almost ten years?

MAX. Whoa.
That is literally my idea of hell.

ZORA. Well –

She slips out of her dress.

Franklin keeps telling me that "Andre has the best pool".
That I "need to just jump in". That I "don't know what I'm missing". Saltwater. Blah blah blah.

She pauses, then walks toward the pool.

BELLAMY. It's really nice!

ZORA. You with an old man too ain't you?

MAX *snorts.*

BELLAMY. What?
(*To* MAX.) Why'd you tell her that?

ZORA. Nobody had to tell me nothing. I can see it all over your
spirit.

ZORA *looks at* BELLAMY *closer. She's almost in the pool
now. Perhaps she has grabbed hold to the handrail.*

But …
Franklin, he –
(*Her feet touch the water.*)
The hell?

BELLAMY. What is it?

ZORA. Is it always this hot?

MAX. Hot?

MAX *walks over and puts his hand in.*

BELLAMY. It's temperature controlled.
During the day
it like,
should be whatever the like
temperature of the ocean is.

MAX. Yeah, it feels normal to me.

ZORA. This feels normal?

ZORA *steps deeper into the water, eyeing it with distrust.*

Huh…

ZORA *looks back.* FRANKLIN, *behind the glass, is lifting
up whatever part of his new doll he has created and is
dancing with it like no one is watching.*

ZORA *takes a big breath then dives deep into the pool.*

Scene Four

FRANKLIN *and* ANDRE *are sitting on a chaise lounge together.* ANDRE *is rubbing* FRANKLIN*'s hair or head as* FRANKLIN *unrolls a Blow Pop.*

FRANKLIN*'s new half-completed doll is hanging out of the slightly open glass door.*

FRANKLIN. I disagree!
    She –
    If like,
    If she…
    (AHH!)
    I'm getting tongue-tied.
    What / I am try–

ANDRE. Because you have nothing to say! For once, you
    realize / that I'm right.

FRANKLIN. No,
    she…
    …
    Carl Andre's work is
    objectively
    less interesting than her work.
    Point blank.
    So to say that like the reason it's more "prudent"
    that someone invest in a
    fucking
    Carl Andre piece
    over an Ana Mendieta piece
    is that
    "he currently holds
    more worth
    in the market"
    is just facile.
    That's lazy.
    I find that to be a bad investment.
    You're investing poorly.
    Because, of course he holds more worth

he's fucking alive.
She isn't.

He begins to lick the Blow Pop.

But when he's dead
no one
will remember him as anything other
than the dude that killed one of the world's / greatest artists.

ANDRE. Oh come on!
That's not fair.

FRANKLIN. And who shat out like
two good poems.
It's not fair that he fucking killed someone and got away
with it.
(I can't believe you would own something of his)

ANDRE. Didn't you say,
"art is worthless when it's owned"?

FRANKLIN *looks at him, confused.*

FRANKLIN. I said that?

ANDRE. Yeah…
Our first night.
…
I asked you to help me find better art for the walls.
And you said:
"art is worthless when it's owned"

FRANKLIN. I was so high that night
I barely / remember

ANDRE (*remembering*). NO!
What you said was,
"art loses its worth the minute it can be owned."

FRANKLIN *sucks hard on the Blow Pop and thinks for a
second.*

FRANKLIN. Well if I did
then like
what I was saying was that –
well yeah –

art
when it's owned
is like…
or… like?
The minute it's no longer being created
and is like heading to a gallery
it's dirty.
Right?
Like that's why like
outsider artists are just
better, or at least more pure.
They like
are free to just create
they don't have to worry
about like
what their art is going to mean
for like
their rent
or like their like
food.
It just is.
It exists because it was made
and for no other reason.

ANDRE *hugs* FRANKLIN *tight. Squeezing him close to his body like a doll. He starts to slowly kiss* FRANKLIN *on his head – slow and unerotic.*

ANDRE. Well Little Naomi,
if you want to be an outsider artist I've got you.
If I'm the only one who ever sees what you do?
That…
I'd have no problem with that.

FRANKLIN *moves away from him, surreptitiously wiping his neck and head.*

FRANKLIN. Well I would.

ANDRE. You would?

FRANKLIN. I think…

ANDRE.…

Smoothly ZORA *walks across the back room looking out to the pool surreptitiously. She locks eyes with* ANDRE *and* FRANKLIN *and gives a small wave.*

FRANKLIN *waves back.*

She exits.

FRANKLIN. It's just –
Yeah!
I don't know?
It's like…

ANDRE. It's like,
"what would my mom think?"
Sorry…
"Mama."

FRANKLIN *looks at him for a moment. He's gotten to the part in the Blow Pop that's unsuckable. He bites into the Blow Pop and begins to chew the gum waiting inside.*

FRANKLIN. What?

ANDRE. I open my home to that woman and she…
The way she looks at me?
That stare?

FRANKLIN. Well, she's difficult.
I told you that she should stay somewhere else.
like…
ugh…
I don't even know why,
what does that / even have to do

ANDRE. Why would you want that?

FRANKLIN. Why?
Because she's my mother.
That's why.
It's been a week I can / tell her –

ANDRE. And you're ashamed.
Of all this.

FRANKLIN. No.
It's

It's not that.
Why would I be?
She –
you guys are saying the same shit and it's whack,
like.
It's not shame.

ANDRE. Then what is it?

…

…

Huh?

…

You've been different since she arrived. She's done
something to you.

FRANKLIN. Different?

ANDRE. Yeah. She's gotten under your skin. You've been
stumbling around in and out of your studio. This is the first
time we've just –
You haven't even touched me since she arrived.

FRANKLIN. I have a lot of work to do. After the show I just –
I hate all the work that Alessia sold and I'm just… I want to
make something new. Different.

ANDRE. And that makes me disgusting to you?

FRANKLIN. No. It's not –
I just need some space.

ANDRE. Space?
What do you mean by space?

FRANKLIN. I don't want to talk about it.

ANDRE. Why?

FRANKLIN. Because I don't.

ANDRE. Franklin…

FRANKLIN *looks up to the sky and takes a deep breath and
then looks at* ANDRE.

He holds his breath, slightly shaking and staring directly at
ANDRE.

Franklin?

ANDRE walks towards FRANKLIN. FRANKLIN *slaps his own face.* ANDRE *stops.*

Staring at ANDRE, FRANKLIN *does it again, this time harder.* ANDRE *reaches for* FRANKLIN.

What are you doing Franklin? Stop!

FRANKLIN *begins slapping his face harder and harder now as* ANDRE *tries to grab for his hands.* ANDRE *grabs his arms and roughly pulls them to his sides.*

FRANKLIN *exhales and spits, the gum flying out of his mouth and into the pool. He starts to slowly breathe normally again.*

What the fuck is wrong with you?

FRANKLIN....
You weren't listening to me, Daddy.
...

FRANKLIN *falls deeper into* ANDRE'*s arms.* FRANKLIN *grabs his face and begins to slowly kiss him, pushing him back towards a chaise.*

ANDRE *looks up at* FRANKLIN *as he falls into the chaise.* FRANKLIN *bends down and kisses* ANDRE *roughly, pulling back with an audible bite. As* ANDRE *wipes away the beginning of what may be blood* FRANKLIN *flashes a smile.*

ANDRE (*wincing*). That was incredibly unnecessary.

FRANKLIN. You're the one who wanted me to touch you.
...
...
Pause.

Do we have any more weed?

ANDRE. I think there's some in the kitchen.

FRANKLIN. Could you roll us a joint?

ANDRE *looks at* FRANKLIN, *he takes him in, processing what just happened.*

I'm fine. I just need to sleep. I'm – like I'm stressing and she's in my head. You're right. I have been different.

ANDRE (*he heads towards the door*). You coming?

FRANKLIN. Yeah just give me a second.

ANDRE....

   ...

   ...

You hate this question
but are you alright?

   ...

   ...

   ...

You've been behaving very oddly lately.
(*He waits for an answer.*)

   ...

   ...

   ...

I love you, Little Naomi.

FRANKLIN....

ANDRE. I love you.
You're mine, I'm yours.
Remember that?

ANDRE *waits a moment for an answer... he exits.*

FRANKLIN *stands by the pool looking out as silence gives way to unfamiliar chords from some far away synthesizer. He looks up and out again at us, his world once again bleeding into ours.*

FRANKLIN *opens his mouth as though he wants to say something to us, but he swallows his words.*

FRANKLIN *looks back to the door where his half-completed doll is lying. He walks over and grabs the half-formed piece and holds it, awkwardly cradling it.*

He begins to hum to it as he rocks back and forth, back and forth.

FRANKLIN (*whispered, to the doll*). I love you. You're mine.

...

You're mine.

Scene Five

FRANKLIN *and* ZORA *sit outside.* ZORA, *on a chaise, watches* FRANKLIN *as he sorts through a pile of XXXL clothes that he tosses onto a nearby chaise lounge.*

The glass door is closed and FRANKLIN'*s large black soft sculpture can be seen three-quarters complete.*

FRANKLIN. – were right,
   you know?
   Like.
   I did make a bunch of "coon babies".
   And it kind of pissed me off
   like
   that I didn't even think of that?
   So I –
   Well that's why
   ...
   I don't know?
   That's where he came from.

ZORA *smiles and gets up to make herself a drink.*

   ...
   What do you think?
   He's...
   Well he's sort of ours...
   I didn't realize it till –
   but
   I wouldn't have come up with him if you hadn't –
   I don't / know...

ZORA *walks over to him and looks at his elbows.*

ZORA. How did you let your skin get this dry?

FRANKLIN. Huh?

ZORA. It's that pool probably. I don't like that pool. It's too hot. Like a damn sauna. Come here.

ZORA *pulls* FRANKLIN *down and rummages through her purse for some cocoa butter. She places him between her legs and starts to rub cocoa butter on his back and arms. She does this in silence for a bit.*

FRANKLIN. Mama?

ZORA. Shhhh… It's real nice hearing your voice every day baby. It. Yeah. It really is.

FRANKLIN. Ha.
   Ok…

ZORA (*finishing up*). You know I'm no good at all this. I'm sure that… I'm sure your anointin' is leading you where you need to be right now. So…

FRANKLIN *stands up and looks at* ZORA *for moment before becoming a total teenager.*

FRANKLIN. Why do you do that, Mama?

ZORA. Do what?

FRANKLIN. I like…
   I start talking about one thing
   and
   like
   obviously I want…
   like, you to –
   I don't know…
   Recognize it?
   Me?
   And like…
   Stay on the fucking topic?
   / And you

ZORA. Hey!

FRANKLIN. You continue to like
    talk bullshit.
    And it's just mean.
    I don't.
    I don't think that like once
    you've even like
    tried to say that you were proud of me
    since you've like been here.
    You just walk around and like, make everyone
    uncomfortable.
    You like look at Andre weird, you're mean to my gallerist…
    and frankly,
    like, I don't give a fuck about my "anointing" or whatever
    the fu–

    ZORA *slaps him and grabs his face. She squeezes his cheeks*
    together with her hands making it almost impossible for him
    to speak.

ZORA. I said "hey". Now I don't know who you "like" think
    you're "like" talking to "like", but YOU KNOW and I KNOW
    that's not how MY SON talks. You ain't "Max" and you ain't
    "Bellamy" and I'm not either one of their mamas. So let's
    check the "bullshits" and the "fucks" at the door. Alright?
    …
    (*She waits for an answer.*)
    …Alright?

FRANKLIN (*through squeezed cheeks*). Yes, ma'am.

ZORA (*still squeezing*). I'm sorry I can't talk to you the way
    you want me to about how great you are, how clever all your
    little ideas are but that's 'cause you ain't great, they ain't
    clever and they weren't yours to begin with.
    …
    …

    Her grip loosens and she starts to caress his face gently.
    FRANKLIN *breathes deeply, slowly.*

FRANKLIN.…thanks, Mama…

ZORA. What I'm tellin' you if you were listening, if you
    remembered how you were raised instead of how you wished

you were, is that we do nothing without the blessings of the Father. You forget that? Humility. Grace. These things before all else. Instead... you up here partying, drinking, doing drugs with Methuselah.

FRANKLIN. I don't do drugs.

ZORA. Don't lie to me...

> FRANKLIN *looks away.*

What happened to the little Franklin that would sit on my lap in the front pew of church and knew every book of the Bible by heart? Who would make little dolls for his Sunday school class and act out little scenes from the Bible? David and Goliath, Samson and Delilah, Doubting Thomas... Used to run around the house pretending to be the ladies in the gospel choir. Singing Shirley Caesar at the top of your lungs. What happened to him? What happened to my baby?

FRANKLIN (*a whine*). I don't know...

   ...

   ...

> *Behind the door we can see* ANDRE *with two packages. He stops before entering, observing the intimate moment.*

ZORA. I think you need to come back home for a little bit.

FRANKLIN. What?
  Why-e?

ZORA. Because I don't know that you're yourself here.

FRANKLIN. Mama, I can't do that.

ZORA. Why don't we pray on it?

FRANKLIN. I don't pray.

ZORA. Let's just pray on it.

> ZORA *grabs* FRANKLIN's *hands and starts to pull him down as:*

ANDRE (*sliding open the door*). He comes bearing gifts!

> ANDRE *awkwardly pushes open the door with his foot the rest of the way.*

ZORA. Actually we were about to pray Andre if you don't
mind...

ANDRE *sets the two packages down*.

ANDRE. Pray?

FRANKLIN *walks over and gives* ANDRE *a kiss*.

FRANKLIN. What did you get us?

ZORA. Franklin we / were...

ANDRE. Was I interrupting something?

FRANKLIN. Mama, later.
(*To* ANDRE.) What is it?

ANDRE *looks from* FRANKLIN *to* ZORA. *He hands* ZORA
a package.

ANDRE. Well...
I wanted to show you, Zora, how much I appreciate both of
you being here.
So I racked my brain, trying to think of what best to get
you...
you're a hard one to shop for.
Hopefully, it will get easier as we,
you know
get to know each other.
But
I called my friend over at Hermès and told him about you
and he said that no woman would be able to resist one of
these
so
I got you one
and a scarf
because "no woman should be without".

ZORA *opens the boxes revealing a very expensive purse*.

FRANKLIN (*through a squeal*). Oh my god.
That's insane.

ZORA *smiles through thin lips*.

ZORA. Yes. Thank you Andre. This is very nice...

ANDRE *looks around nervously.*

ANDRE. Oh no, you don't like the color do you?

FRANKLIN (*torn*). Don't be silly, it's a Birkin.
She / loves it.

ZORA. I have a purse. The color is fine. But I have a purse. So I said thank you, but...

FRANKLIN. (Oh my god)

ANDRE....

FRANKLIN. What about me?
What did I get?
I'm easy to impress.

ZORA *looks over and away.*

ANDRE (*handing him a box*). Well based on our conversation the other night, I almost got you a Mendieta. Haha. But it wouldn't have gotten here by this afternoon. So...

FRANKLIN *excitedly tears open a box as* ANDRE *slowly bends down.* FRANKLIN *freezes when he sees what's inside. He drops it and slowly backs away. He exits through the sliding doors.*

ANDRE *looks around, confused.* ZORA *walks over and picks up the box. The chords from before begin to play softly, slowly crescendoing as the scene ends.*

ZORA. Why'd you get him this?

ANDRE. What just happened?

ZORA. Why did you get him this?

ANDRE. Zora, excuse me but I / need to go find Franklin.

ZORA. No. Excuse me. I asked you a question. Why, did you get him this?

ANDRE. Because I love him. That's why.

ZORA. Look at me. In my eyes.

He does.

Tell me what you "love". What is it EXACTLY? Because I don't feel it.

ANDRE. It's not for you to feel. It's for him.

ZORA. No. That boy in there is mine. That's my baby. His whole life I felt what he feels. In here. And I don't feel love. Here right now. I don't. It's something else. Something / different.

We feel FRANKLIN'*s presence, his ears on them both.*

ANDRE (*choosing his words carefully*). Zora, you're very upset. Obviously.
I should have talked to you more before today, I'm sorry.
You make me uncomfortable,
in my own home, you make me uncomfortable.
Maybe it's because seeing you is like seeing a deep part of him
a part he hasn't shown me yet.
But what you need to know is that he will,
he's shown me parts of Franklin you haven't seen,
can't see.
Things I can't unsee and that I can't articulate.
Things that make you vibrate in their presence.
Electric.
…
…
…
I just want to go talk to Franklin.
I want to end this
and go to him.
I'm not competing with you. This isn't a competition.

ZORA (*pointing at him*). That right there. See. You can't even say what it is. You'd rather finance his affections than name your own. I'll go see what's wrong / with him.

ANDRE. He has this little spot!
That I saw,
I felt,
when I first met him that slowly I've burrowed my way into.
It's warm
and it's bright.

And I don't know if I'm big enough to fill it but I love the
fact that it's there.
I love that I get to try.

ZORA stares at ANDRE *for a moment breathing in this
moment of honesty.*

ZORA. You think he saw a spot like that in you?
Huh?

ANDRE....
I don't know.

ZORA. And you don't care.
And that's the problem.

ZORA hands ANDRE *the box before she exits.*

*ANDRE sits down, looking at the box in his hand. He sets it
down on the chaise.*

End of Act Two.

ACT THREE (FRANKLIN)

Scene One

*The haunting chords from before continue to play as the lights
slowly rise, first from the pool then from* FRANKLIN*'s studio
behind the glass doors, where* FRANKLIN *sits finishing his
sculpture surrounded by the* GOSPEL CHOIR *looking on.*

FRANKLIN *diligently attaches a head to his soft sculpture
doppelgänger before standing him up and leaving the room. He
returns with another sculpture shaped like his mother before
placing her next to the wall and leaving again to grab a large,
white, featureless sculpture that we can assume is Andre.*

The GOSPEL CHOIR *sways back and forth to the rhythm of the
chords as they begin to, almost imperceptibly, sing a song with
no words. Not that we would be able to hear them, the doors are
closed.*

FRANKLIN *positions the Zora sculpture next to the Andre
sculpture as though they are sleeping. He stares at them for a
while. Then he places the Franklin sculpture at their feet in the
fetal position. His hand at his mouth as though sucking on his
thumb.*

The GOSPEL CHOIR *raises their hands like they are praising
the Lord.*

FRANKLIN *then places the Zora doll head next to the Andre
doll head and smushes them around, forcing them to kiss. He
grabs the Franklin doll and makes his hand clap.*

The GOSPEL CHOIR *begins to clap as well, moving around
like the tempo has gotten quicker even though the chord is still
moving at the same haunting pace.* FRANKLIN *grabs the
Andre doll and throws him on his stomach. He sets the Zora
doll on a table to watch. He picks up the Franklin doll and
places him behind the Andre doll. He forces the Franklin doll to
violently thrust into the Andre doll, over and over and over
again. Then* FRANKLIN *picks up the Franklin doll and has*

him slap the Andre doll. Then he slowly pulls the Franklin doll to the glass and presses his body into the doll's body as they slowly move across the glass until finally they collapse.

FRANKLIN *looks over and sees the box on the chaise.* FRANKLIN *pulls a ring out of the box. He looks at the big Franklin and gasps, surprised.*

FRANKLIN (*to the sculpture*). I love you!
　You're mine…

He kisses the sculpture then puts on the ring. At that moment, ANDRE walks in and looks down at FRANKLIN on the floor.

ANDRE. Franklin?

FRANKLIN *looks up through glistening eyes.*

FRANKLIN.…Yes, Daddy?
　Yes!
　Yes Daddy!

FRANKLIN *looks up and begins to giggle uncontrollably.*

He grabs ANDRE's hand and pulls him into him, giggling and smiling, too tickled to even kiss.

Scene Two

It's late. Nobody is outside. The pool sits there glistening in the late-night light. In the background we can see FRANKLIN's new larger soft sculptures now dressed in formalwear.

Then we hear the sound of a phone ringing. It's there, glowing by the pool: RING RING RING.

The ring wanders around the theatre, stumbling into the walls until finally we hear:

BEEP!

FRANKLIN (*voice-over*). Hi, you've reached Franklin.
　Sorry I uh,
　I can't get to the phone right now.

But if you need anything just leave a message
Or, like, send me an email
or a text
and I'll get back to you at my earliest convenience.
Um…
Thank you.

BEEP!

Silence. Perhaps the sound of some breath from far off, but overwhelmingly silent.

BEEP!

The lights in the white room come on. And a tipsy ANDRE and FRANKLIN walk outside to the pool. As they shut the door FRANKLIN starts undressing to skinny dip.

ANDRE. How excited are you?

FRANKLIN*'s moved from teen to child now…*

FRANKLIN. I just want to get wet.

ANDRE. Franklin
take a second to process
exactly
what is happening right now.

FRANKLIN *jumps in the pool.*

FRANKLIN. You take a second!

ANDRE *looks down and starts to take off his shoes.*

ANDRE. Getting an international follow-up to your
first solo show with a –
well it's huge.
That's –
You should be freaking out right now.

FRANKLIN *splashes him with a big wave of water. Then puts his thumb in his mouth.*

Not on these, Franklin!
Fuck.
These are suede.

FRANKLIN. Sorry.

FRANKLIN *takes his thumb out of his mouth then splashes*
ANDRE *again.*

ANDRE. Franklin.
Stop this.
This is unacceptable.

ANDRE *picks up his shoes and inspects the damage.*

FRANKLIN. You wanna spank me?
huh?
Fiaaaaannnncéé.
(*In "Single Ladies" rhythm.*) Oh oh oh oh oh oh
oh oh oh oh…

FRANKLIN *smiles before he throws more water, connecting,
once again, with the shoes.* ANDRE *jumps back.*

After a moment, ANDRE *takes off the rest of his clothes,
throws the shoes by the side of the pool and jumps in. He
swims to* FRANKLIN *and grabs him. Pulling his face close
to his own.*

Then, abruptly, he begins walking out of the pool, a wet
FRANKLIN *in his arms. He throws* FRANKLIN *onto a
chaise on his stomach and holds him down with a knee. He
reaches down, grabs one of his suede shoes, and brings it
down forcefully on* FRANKLIN*'s backside.*

Ow.

ANDRE. Apologize.

FRANKLIN *looks up and laughs a bit.* ANDRE *begins hitting
him harder, the sound of the WHOP! as wet as* FRANKLIN.

With every syllable he brings the shoe down. FRANKLIN
convulsing about in rhythm to his beating.

I
Said
TO
A –
POL –
O –
GIZE /

TO
ME.

FRANKLIN. FUCK! OW!

ANDRE. SO
  FUCK
  ING
  A –
  POL
  O –
  GIZE
  NOW!

On "now" the shoe flies out of ANDRE's *hand, so forceful were his hits.*

FRANKLIN *may be crying, he may not, but he's definitely shaking. That wasn't a good spanking.*

FRANKLIN. I apologize.

ANDRE *picks up the other shoe and slaps him again hard, once.*

ANDRE. Who are you apologizing to?

FRANKLIN. I apologize, Daddy.

ANDRE *hits him again.*

ANDRE. Apologize for what?

FRANKLIN. I apologize for splashing you with water, Daddy.

ZORA *can be seen in the room behind them staring out.*
ANDRE *hits* FRANKLIN.

ANDRE. That's not why.

FRANKLIN. I apologize for splashing you with water and ruining your suede shoes Daddy.

ANDRE (*hitting him as he talks*). That's not it either.

Again the phone begins to ring: RING RING RING.

FRANKLIN *looks up at* ANDRE, *who looks back at* FRANKLIN. FRANKLIN *reaches over for his phone.*

Who is it?

FRANKLIN. Blocked.

ANDRE. Ignore it.

> FRANKLIN *looks down at the phone. He hits "send to voicemail".*

> *BEEP!*

FRANKLIN (*voice-over*). Hi, you've reached Franklin.
Sorry I uh,
I can't get to the phone right now.
But if you need anything just leave a message
Or, like, send me an email
or a text
and I'll get back to you at my earliest convenience.
Um...
Thank you...

> *BEEP!*

> *The sound of a thin inhalation is heard. Slowly* ZORA *exits before she is seen in the white room.*

ANDRE. Are you sure you're ready for tomorrow?

> FRANKLIN *looks at him without a word.*

...I need to know that / you are...

FRANKLIN. Daddy tell me a story.

ANDRE. I need to know that you –

FRANKLIN. I'll tell you one.

ANDRE. Franklin, / I –

FRANKLIN. Mama thinks,
that when he came I don't remember.
But I do.
I do remember.
I was upstairs,
in my room,
and I was watching out the window when he drove up
and got out the car.

He was.
He was tall… but he won't like
real tall?
He was like tall enough.
And he was real gray.
And he told her that he wanted to see me.
And she said "no"
She said, "He's good.
You're so ugly.
That baby is good
he's mine,
he don't need you."
And he said, "But I need him"
I think.
I couldn't really hear, but
I think
I think that's what he said.
He said, "But I need him".
And she said a bad word…
She called him a bad word
and so he left.
(*He takes a moment.*)
And when he left I said it.
The bad word.
I looked outside and opened my window
and I said,
"That's right,
I don't need you,
I don't need you
you ugly 'do nothing nigga'."
And I closed up the window.
I shut it tight.
And then I started playing with my dolls.

FRANKLIN *stands up and yawns and starts to put his clothes back on.*

I'm sorry for splashin' you, Daddy.
I'm –
I'm gonna go up to bed.

FRANKLIN *exits.* ANDRE *sits, considering* FRANKLIN's *story as the lights slowly fade.*

Scene Three

An early morning sun dances over the pool, little crystals seem to dance upon the water like diamonds before ZORA, *who is on her knees at the pools edge, praying.*

ZORA. Father,
  you
  and you alone
  know why you test us the way you do,
  why you place before us demons and spirits in our path
  who hold jewels like none our eyes have ever beheld
  who spin keys before us that open doors you've told us
  should be locked till morrow.
  I know this Lord.
  I know it like I know you made the air for me to breathe
  and the eyes through which I see.
  But I'm here before you,
  humble,
  and at my end
  asking that you reveal a bit of your divine plan to me
  so that I won't feel so lost today, O Lord...
  You spoke to me Father.
  You spoke
  and you told me,
  "Go."
  And I did.
  I came.
  And you spoke more,
  you said,
  "Look"
  And I did.
  And I saw.
  Lord did I see.
  I saw and saw more than I thought I would, could, shoulda
  seen
  but I did it Lord
  because you were speaking to me, through me Lord.
  But you've been quiet these past few days.
  Silent.
  ...

...
...
I don't know Lord.
Maybe you been speaking.
Just too soft?
...
Can you speak up?
Yell a bit?
The Devil,
he screaming.
Every morning, day, night he screaming.
I know the sun and the stars are your province Lord
but here,
in this place
it feels like the Sunshine is a megaphone for the Devil Lord:
And I can't hear myself think,
let alone hear you speak,
so I need you to yell out Lord.
Yell out from the most high
and tell me what I need to do.
Cuz something done grabbed hold of my boy Lord
and I need your help casting it out.
I need you Lord.
This city a legion running through my baby's body
in his blood
his bones
and even with all this water here to drown them
I don't see no sheep I can curse with his affliction.
He ain't speaking to me Lord in his voice
He speaking in a voice I remember but don't recognize.

In suit pants and no shirt, just an untied tie, FRANKLIN
*enters and looks over to his mother. Even in a suit everything
about him feels all of eight years old.*

So Lord I'm asking,
begging,
that you speak to me right now...
Tell me / what you woul–

FRANKLIN. Mama?
Mommy?

*ZORA looks back at him with tear-stained eyes. FRANKLIN
holds part of the untied tie towards her.*

ZORA. Franklin?

FRANKLIN. Mama?
  I gotta –
  Will you do the tie for me?
  I wanna –
  I gotta practice the tie
  and I wanna
  I need you to show me first.

*ZORA looks up, unsure if this is the answer to the prayer
she'd been praying.*

ZORA. Why you wanna do the tie right now baby?

FRANKLIN. Because if I don't do it now,
  try it,
  I won't be able to do it later
  and I don't want everyone to be mad at me.
  I don't –
  It's –
  I have to wear a tie.
  You wear ties.
  I gotta wear one.

*ZORA gets off her knees. She slowly walks over and looks at
FRANKLIN. She takes him in. For a long moment before
she slowly begins to tie the tie.*

ZORA. You ain't asked me to do this for you in a long time.

FRANKLIN. It's cuz I don't have to wear them.
  I'm an artist.
  Artists don't wear ties.
  We're too poor.

FRANKLIN laughs at his own joke.

ZORA. Yeah…

  …

  She continues to tie.

Let me ask you something Franklin.

FRANKLIN. Yes ma'am?

She finishes with the tie.

ZORA. First, you like it?

FRANKLIN *walks over to the pool and looks down at his reflection.*

FRANKLIN. You did it real good, Mama, thank you.

ZORA. You're welcome baby.
   …
   …
   Franklin, baby…
   tell me bout the sex.

FRANKLIN *looks up from the pool, disgusted.*

FRANKLIN. The what?

ZORA. The sex.
   Tell me about it.
   It must be good if you so in love.

FRANKLIN. Ew Mom!
   Gross.

ZORA. Nah you grown, I'm grown. And I wanna know.
   how he makes you feel.
   I remember how good it can feel to be held by somebody old
   somebody wrinkled.
   Your skin feels tighter in their hands
   like it'll never let loose of your bones
   and you get tight all over
   everywhere
   and they can feel it too.
   And you can feel them feel it
   and it makes you feel invincible
   because what they're feeling ain't your beauty…
   it's your life that seems everlasting in their eyes.
   …
   So tell me bout the sex.
   Do it make you feel invincible?

Like you breathe deeper and harder than anyone else?
What does it do to you Franklin?
Do your knees buckle?
You feel faint?
Tell me Franklin.
Tell me.
What is it that Methuselah do that rile you up so much?
How does he have you walking around here about four
degrees from stup/id ev–

FRANKLIN *is trembling and looking away.* ZORA *stops
and listens.*

God's silence is like a foghorn.

…
Baby.
You look handsome today.

FRANKLIN. Thank you.

ZORA. You're my handsome boy.
    You know that?

FRANKLIN. Thank you.

ZORA. You know I love you.
    You're mine.
    You know that right?

FRANKLIN. Thank you.

ZORA. I love you.

FRANKLIN. I love you.

ZORA. No you do/n't.

    FRANKLIN *is gone.* ZORA *is alone.*

Scene Four

FRANKLIN *stands alone in the pool, amniotic fluid.*

The GOSPEL CHOIR *is there and a pageant begins: The chaise lounges move offstage, replaced by a dining-room table and chairs. They move to the side of the pool once* MAX, BELLAMY, *and* ALESSIA *are done.*

A banner reads: "ANDRE + FRANKLIN" and FRANKLIN*'s new dolls loom large around them.*

The table settings are immaculate with colorful cakes and treats sprinkled upon white linen.

FRANKLIN *eyes wander over it all until they lock with* ANDRE*'s and he is hit by an immense wave.*

FRANKLIN *and* ANDRE*'s wedding march begins, taking them to the heads of the table,* FRANKLIN *sucking his thumb.* ZORA *enters, staring at this luscious scene, and sits in the middle of the table wearing a long black dress. She has had three glass of champagne. On one side sits* BELLAMY *and* MAX *talking to* ANDRE, *on the other is* ALESSIA, *talking to* FRANKLIN. ZORA *is silently tipsy.*

A phone rings. They all look up, except FRANKLIN *who looks at us. It ends abruptly. Dropped call.*

ALESSIA. They love that you've gone macro.
    Love it.
    They really
    really do.
    Now we just have to figure out how you want to package it.
    Any ideas?
    …
    …
    …
    Well…
    I have a lot of ideas.
    I was thinking about you
    and
    largesse
    and

blackness
and
queerness
You know…
in relationship to this current moment
in a way?
It's –
like –
Women
African-Americans
We are finally pushing aside
the white cishet
blowhard art bros of the past
and just, like,
proclaiming it, right?
THIS IS OUR TIME
WE ARE HERE.
WE CAN TAKE UP SPACE TOO.
We can be outlandish
and brazen
and unsafe
and careless
and all those other things the big boys have been able to be
forever.
Literally
It's so pop.
It's so Gaga.
You might as well name the piece:
"#SuddenlyTheKoonsIsMe."
What you think about that?

FRANKLIN….

ALESSIA. I know
I know.
Today is not a day for work.
It's just –
it's
Really beautiful.
Really challenging work Franklin.

BELLAMY *is showing* ANDRE *and* MAX *something on her phone*.

BELLAMY. I'm so happy I didn't wear this…
    I mean.
    Right?
    I look horrible.
    Geoff thought I looked fine
    but
    you can't argue with a well-shot selfsnap you know?

ANDRE. Who's Geoff?

BELLAMY. Geoff.

MAX. Some new guy.

BELLAMY. Geoff's not new.

MAX. He's not?

BELLAMY. You're such an asshole sometimes Max.

ZORA (*under her breath*). Don't talk to your brother that way
    Bellamy. (Language.)

    *ANDRE looks over at ZORA who is still looking out,
    disinterested.*

    The phone rings out again. Everyone looks up. FRANKLIN
    looks to us, then to ANDRE, *desperate. Dropped call.*

ANDRE. Should we get started?

    He reaches for a glass of champagne. ZORA *looks at him
    pointedly.*

ZORA. What are you doing?

ANDRE. I was just going to get the speeches started.

ZORA. Hm…

    ZORA *looks over to* FRANKLIN *who continues to suck on
    his thumb. He makes a face. He slumps down into his seat.*
    ZORA *turns to* MAX, *who is clinking his knife into his glass.*

MAX. Well I guess since
    I would like,
    be best man if this were like a normal
    whatever
    …

I'm best man so I should say my speech first.

BELLAMY *and* ALESSIA *laugh.*

I –
yeah.
Like…
This whole thing has been like,
a mindfuck to me.
…
…
It's cool though, I mean…
Yay!
(*He turns to* ANDRE.)
Ok, so like,
Franklin and I have been –
he's been my best friend since like
he first moved to LA.
…
…
He was working, uh
at this like
art gallery?
In Santa Monica.
And his boss would
like
he was like this gross straight dude.
And he would like
pull his dick out at parties and like
would hang out with porn stars
and I'm sure he was a criminal
or something
because I don't think any art was ever
like
nothing was sold before Franklin got there.
So I don't know how the lights stayed on but…
Like, I would go to Jacob's,
this dude,
I would go to his parties a lot,
because they were good
and the art on the walls was always the same
for three years straight

the same
But then
like one day Franklin was there
and he was like,
Jacob,
he was like...
"This dude right here?
He's gonna make me rich."
And then he like offered me G and walked away.
And Franklin just sort of
stood there
And laughed like he didn't hear it
Or like
he wouldn't hear it?
Or something...
And like,
literally,
I only ever went to Jacob's,
like
I only went to those parties because,
like,
that was my scene
or whatever
but like
then,
Franklin was like:
"Wanna see some new stuff?"
And he took me into this massive room,
some hidden MASSIVE room
that he had hidden away
under his nose
he had created a cavern
for just himself...
that was filled with these toys
it looked like
toys...
And it was the first time I saw that art could be this
like game, this fun game or something?
And like
that this dude was fucking fun.
And he wanted to have fun with me?

And this dude,
this –
Franklin
He could keep a secret
and he wanted to keep one with me.
And that's when I fell in love with him,
that's when I –
But ...
Yeah,
I don't know ...
anyway.
Here's to more fun?
Years of it.
More fun!

ANDRE *stares at him.* MAX *stares back and takes a drink.*
Everyone claps except ZORA.

ANDRE. Max everybody.
Thank you Max.
Bellamy?

BELLAMY. Me?
Oh.
I didn't write anything.
So...

ZORA *looks over at* BELLAMY *sternly.*

ZORA. You got plenty to say though.
You better get it on out now girl.
Get it out.

BELLAMY (*to* ZORA). Um...
Yes ma'am.
...
...
...I –

The phone rings again. Everybody looks up. FRANKLIN
looks to BELLAMY *then begins to suck his thumb*
vigorously, trying to drown out the ring. It abruptly stops.

Time moves weird here.
Have any of you ever felt that?

Or is it like
just me
and Franklin?
Because
yeah...
like
We could've been living here
as best friends
for the past six months
or the past
six decades
and emotionally
it like,
there'd sort of be
like
no difference?
No like
real difference?
You know?
Because of the sun.
The guy I'm seeing?
Geoff
He –
He really tried to get what I was saying
when I told him.
He was like, "Oh yeah...
I see"
But I could tell he didn't really get it.
And what
I think that
Or like
what's at the bottom of this is that
if it's summer every day
when even is it?
You know?
Just think about that.
If it's summer every day
when even is it?
Franklin asked me that
When we first met
And I've never forgotten it because it made it feel like we
had found a magical land.

We were at I think
one of the first parties
after he left the art gallery job?
And I was
so in love with this person who
I was becoming more than friends with
because I could feel a bond
growing that felt familial immediately. Deep love.
Not friendship.
Familyship.
I wrote it in my journal.
"When it's summer every day
when even is it?"

…

…

…

So I don't know how long I've been here
how long we've been
friends
but it feels like a long time
and a short time
at the same time.
And I feel like
just since you've been here
I felt a whole life of a family
happen between and around us
and I've never seen you
more productive
and happy in our
entire familyship.
So here's to the newest member of our
family?
To more timeless days with you
and Franklin, Daddy.

Once again everyone claps except ZORA. ANDRE *wipes a
tear from his eye and* ZORA *watches, incredulous.*

ANDRE (*to* FRANKLIN). Franklin?
    Wasn't that beautiful?
    "To more timeless days"…
    You're a poet Bellamy.
    Thank you.

ZORA's done. She can't anymore. She stands up raising her glass.

ZORA. If you all will indulge me for a moment...
    I...

She gestures towards her son and his eyes meet hers. He begins a smile that slowly fades as she continues:

Yeah
I just can't go on without us
at least
attempting
to bless this union.
Since no one wanted to go to a church.
Call a pastor,
we should wait a second.
Do this proper.
So everybody,
just
if you don't mind...
lower your heads.

They do, ANDRE *taking a breath.*

FRANKLIN *looks around as though willing a phone to ring again. It doesn't. No ring. He begins to breathe deeper, more strained.*

FRANKLIN (*through gritted teeth*). I don't pray.

ZORA. Dear Heavenly Father
    thank you for bringing all of us here today
    to celebrate you.
    To bask in your glory
    and commune with each other as
    Franklin and Andre attempt to make some semblance of a
    life together.

ZORA *opens her eyes and looks at* ANDRE *who never closed his.* FRANKLIN *begins to shake his head. This is all too much. Will the phone ring again? Please?*

With an intake of breath the dolls begin to loom larger around them and the GOSPEL CHOIR *begins to march towards the table – a cacophony of vocalizing and harmonizing – as* ZORA *opens and closes her mouth in slow motion, emphatically speaking as no words come out.*

Everyone but FRANKLIN *seems to hear what she is saying. He sits, sucking his thumb vigorously, trying to shut off all the sounds in his head until he's not.*

FRANKLIN (*loudly*). I SAID I DON'T PRAY!

ZORA (*with no sound*). ~~How dare you?~~
    ~~You're a ruiner.~~
    ~~Who ruins a prayer?~~
    ~~I'll tell you: a ruiner.~~
    ~~Oh Lord above save me from myself~~
    ~~before anger leaves my tongue~~
    ~~and enters my hands~~
    ~~Lord.~~
    ~~RUINER!~~

FRANKLIN *looks to* ANDRE, *willing him to speak, willing him to drown out this noise with his eyes.*

ZORA *freezes mid-speech.*

FRANKLIN *looks over to* ANDRE, *willing him to speak again.*

ANDRE. Alright Franklin
    I understand now
    I understand
    this is what she does to you
    she freezes you,
    Makes you feel small.
    Like the dolls you played with in your
    room
    all those hours
    all those nights.
    But I can make her leave.
    Like your father.
    I can make her leave like she made him leave.
    Would you like that Franklin?
    Would you?

He nods his head yes. ZORA *unfreezes.*

Suddenly FRANKLIN *is seeing* ANDRE *and* ZORA *just as
he had seen* ZORA *and that not-too-tall, not-too-short man
so long ago from his bedroom window.*

(*In another's voice.*) No!
HE'S GOOD.
YOU'RE SO UGLY
THAT BABY IS GOOD ZORA!
HE'S MINE!
HE DON'T NEED YOU!
THIS BABY DON'T NEED YOU!

FRANKLIN *keeps looking out and fear moves through his
body and into his eyes. He loses all the color a black boy can
lose.*

ZORA. BUT I NEED HIM.

ANDRE (*in another's voice*). He don't need you!
What he need a
ugly do nothin' nigga for?

*The phone begins to ring again, longer, more sustained…
Everyone looks up. Dropped call.*

FRANKLIN *looks between his mother and* ANDRE *then
starts to cry and tries to say something but nothing comes out.*

GOSPEL CHOIR (*operatic*).
    THAT'S ALL YOU WANTED!

ZORA. "But I need him?"
Franklin?
That ain't how it went.

FRANKLIN *looks at the audience and collapses in on
himself. The Franklin doll looming above him.*

ANDRE *and* ZORA *turn towards the Franklin doll sharply
before turning towards each other.*

The others watch on like it's theatre.

GOSPEL CHOIR (*operatic*).
    THAT'S ALL YOU WANTED!

ANDRE (*in another's voice*). Zora!

ZORA (*younger*). Who are you yelling at?

ANDRE (*in another's voice*). Let me in.

ZORA (*younger*). Uh uh,
    no
    we ain't doin' that
    you don't get to walk up in here
    and
    demand to see that baby
    after / you just –

ANDRE (*in another's voice*). I'm his daddy
    I can do whatever / the hell I want.

ZORA (*younger*). No you aren't.
    I am.
    I been his daddy
    since
    you threw a handful of
    twenties at me
    and told me
    to go figure my situation out.
    MY SITUATION.
    So I figured it out.
    We figured it out.
    Me and Franklin.

ANDRE (*in another's voice*). Lil girl
    move out the way.
    I'm not playing with your fast ass
    no more.
    I wanna see how much of me he got in him.

ZORA (*younger*). Well get to movin' 'cause
    He ain't got nothing of yours
    'cause you don't have nothing to give him.
    Why you here?
    So you can leave
    and forget him again?
    Forget us again?
    Uh uh.
    I know what that feels like
    what it does to you.
    You're not breaking him apart like that.

ANDRE (*in another's voice*). Lil girl I didn't break you
you were broke when you arrived.
And I'm not gonna do nothing to that / boy –

ZORA (*younger*). Even when you're doing nothing
you're doing it wrong!
How often do you see your others?

ANDRE (*in another's voice*). That ain't none of your business,
Zora.
I wanna see the boy
see how much of me he got on his face.
Lord help him if he end up
with too much of you on him.

ZORA (*younger*). No!
He's good
and
he has none of you on his face.
None!
You're so ugly
And he's beautiful.
So so beautiful.
That baby is good
and he's mine.
This baby don't need you.
'Cause you an ugly do nothin' nigga!
Prove to me that you
capable of doing
something
anything
for this boy
and you can see him all you want
but till then?

A phone begins to ring, they all look up. The call drops.

Everyone looks at FRANKLIN.

The water in the pool begins to boil.

ALESSIA (*in another's voice*). You a ugly do nothin' nigga.

MAX (*in another's voice*). You a ugly do nothin' nigga.

BELLAMY (*in another's voice*). You a ugly do nothin' nigga.

ZORA (*in another's voice*). You a ugly do nothin' nigga.

ANDRE (*in another's voice*). You a ugly do nothin' nigga.

GOSPEL CHOIR.
> DADDY WON'T NOTHIN' BUT A SHHHHHH
> DADDY WON'T NOTHIN' BUT A SHHHHHH
> DADDY WON'T NOTHIN' BUT A SHHHHHH

FRANKLIN (*slapping himself*). I'm an ugly do nothin' nigga
> I'm an ugly do nothin' nigga
> I'm an ugly do nothin' nigga
> I'm an ugly do nothin' nigga.

The phone rings again and everyone looks up.

FRANKLIN *begins to shake and shiver, his hand slowly moving up his chest to his throat. The call drops. And the dolls fall away.*

Everyone looks back at FRANKLIN.

ZORA. Franklin,
> Baby.
> Look at me.

ANDRE. Franklin are you alright?

FRANKLIN *is still shaking, shivering, not sure what layer of reality he's in. He looks out but just sees the pool.*

FRANKLIN. I need water.

ZORA. Water baby?
> Ok…
> Max?

ZORA *turns to receive a glass from* MAX *and* FRANKLIN *bursts into a temper tantrum.*

FRANKLIN. NO!
> Daddy, give me the water!
> I want Daddy to give me the water!
> Daddy?

ANDRE. Of course, son!

ZORA *moves to grab* FRANKLIN*'s flailing limbs as*
ANDRE, *without hesitation, moves toward the table to hand*
FRANKLIN *a glass.* ZORA *looks from her son to* ANDRE.

With an inhalation, she's a preacher. The table her pulpit.

ZORA. You're ignorant!
  Let me tell you something:
  To father a black child
  is to see the majesty of your
  seed's promise
  erased with his first breath.
  The moment
  you see his melanin crystallize
  you see him die.
  Why do you think so many of them leave?
  The daddies?
  It's not conditioning.
  It ain't slavery.
  That don't make much sense once you really dig down deep
  into it.
  It's the realization that
  even their male-ness
  can't brighten up
  the utter darkness
  of their child's future.
  The only reason the mothers stay
  is because
  we're prepared.
  We've
  been promised darkness since the day
  we looked down and saw blood looming
  black and scarlet
  in the lining of our
  lil two-dollar panties.

SPLASH!

FRANKLIN, *still shaking and shivering, walks into the pool,*
thumb in his mouth.

BELLAMY. Franklin!

BELLAMY, ALESSIA *and* MAX *run towards the pool.*
ANDRE *and* ZORA *look up from their tussle and into the pool.*

MAX. Ms Zora!

ALESSIA *begins to back away just as* ZORA *snaps at her.*

ZORA (*to* ALESSIA). My Bible…
my purse.

ALESSIA *turns and looks for a purse then grabs a pocket Bible from inside it and hands it to* ZORA, *who makes her way to the pool.*

Bellamy help me with his arms
Max the legs.

They obey and all three begin wading their way into the pool as ANDRE *stares on, horrified by* FRANKLIN.

As ZORA *walks to* FRANKLIN *she begins grabbing hold of him with a mother's might. When she arrives:*

The Lord said…
in Ephesians,
Chapter six
Verse ten
I believe…
"Finally,
be strong in the Lord
and in the strength of his might.
Put on the whole armor of God,
that you may be able to stand against the schemes of the
Devil.
For we do not wrestle against flesh and blood,
but against the rulers,
against the authorities,
against the cosmic powers over this present darkness,
against the spiritual forces of evil
in the heavenly places."

ANDRE. Zora!
Zora this ends now!

ZORA *just looks at him.* MAX *and* BELLAMY *have*
FRANKLIN's *appendages as* ZORA *starts trying to lift him,*
before:

ZORA. I can't think of a more heavenly place
than where I'm standing right now.
I'm not leaving without my baby.

ANDRE *rushes into the pool, frightened of what* ZORA *may*
be doing.

ZORA, BELLAMY *and* MAX *pull* FRANKLIN *flat, before:*

In the name of the Father!

ZORA *looks towards the sky and begins to whisper*
something. She takes FRANKLIN *and pushes him deep into*
the water just as ANDRE *grabs hold to him as well.*

Everyone freezes. And before FRANKLIN *emerges from the*
water a little miracle happens. Maybe it snows for a moment
in Bel Air.

FRANKLIN *comes up from the water and looks out at the*
audience. He pants, catching his breath, looking at them.

Blackout.

Scene Five

MAX, BELLAMY, *and* ANDRE *are sitting at a dining table*
beneath a banner that reads: "FRANKLIN".

FRANKLIN, *wearing the Speedo and towel from the first scene,*
walks back outside. He walks past ALESSIA, *who is in the*
white room on the phone with the dolls, then up to the table and
grabs a glass. He has the confidence of an adult again.

He smiles at ZORA. ZORA *doesn't react.*

FRANKLIN *looks at his mother and wills her to speak. She*
doesn't.

FRANKLIN. "You're so ugly."
That's the title.
"You're. So. Ugly."
Because
That's what I used to think all the time
and not just because you told me I looked like him, Mama.
Because it was a fact.
The fact that you SAID I looked like him is what made it
hurt even more.
Made me hate you even more Mama.
Because you chose him.
Some ugly ass nigga
and you gave me his ugly.
Whatever that even looked like.
All I knew is that some part of his ugly looked like me.
You had said.
...
"You're so ugly..."
...
...
...
I really hate him.
When I was little
I used to dream that Captain Planet would find him, tie him
up and leave him somewhere horrible.
Somewhere I'd never be
so I wouldn't be forced to look at every man
with a nose shaped like mine
or ears that point in the same way
and wonder
"are you my father?"
Because the only image of him I had to go
on was the back of his head
on our driveway
from a window
that felt a mile away.

He looks out to us and says this directly to us, tears almost in his eyes:

Like my ultimate fantasy
Is to get as big as the artists Andre has on the walls here.

And then do a performance piece where I compel my
audience to find my father probably in some dilapidated city
like
Detroit or Houston
or some other generally horrible place
and then this audience will make an almost snuff film
of them like torturing my dad.
Maybe this is that piece?
Or paint some great, grand painting,
and like, after my death some art restorer
with digital imaging software will see that there's another
painting beneath it and like,
that painting has detailed instructions on how and where they
can find my father's body to exhume it and how to reanimate
it so he can
mourn my passing and his newfound loneliness in a dark
future that's been shaped by my work.
My ultimate fantasy is my father seeing my birth a thousand
times over on repeat,
a video in my retrospective, and at the moment when he feels
that inhalation of pride I've read a father is supposed to feel
upon seeing his child kick his feet, I'll stab him in the chest
and watch him bleed.

He laughs. BELLAMY *and* MAX *shift uncomfortably in
their chairs, unable to speak.*

Mama,
Mama what you think about that huh?
What did you think of my show?
I'm listening.

After a moment, ZORA *stands up and grabs her purse.*

ZORA. I think I've stayed too long baby.
That's what I think.

FRANKLIN. What?

ZORA. I think I spent too long thinking that just because I had
you, you were mine.
And you were,
For a time...
but somewhere,

Somewhere along the way you became his

…

(*This cuts her as she says it*.) Weak.

Like him.

Like that moment when I told him about you.

How you were a blessing?

Weak.

I –

When I came here

I thought,

it was

(*She gestures around*.)

I thought this was your shift.

The glamor,

the money,

your white friends,

this white man,

I thought…

My Lord.

I needed to think…

Was blinded by my need to think

it was all of them

that they had seduced you away from me…

from your past

from yourself.

But it was you…

It was him…

What made you look at me like you hated me when I arrived.

You've been hiding the him in you, somewhere in your spirit

for so long… so deep in some hole that he must have just

been wooed out in the sunshine unbeknownst to me back

home.

I'm leaving baby.

FRANKLIN. What?

I don't hate you Mama.

I love you.

ZORA. You look at me like you don't.

…

…

You're on your own, baby.

ZORA *begins to walk to the door.*

FRANKLIN. But Mama. No
No –
I don't.
Please don't say that.
I want this for you
I want this for us.
I made this for you.
I made this for us.
I see how you / could –

ZORA. You don't see nothing, baby.
If you saw past your nose you'd be running out of here
behind me.
But you ain't going nowhere.
This how you living now.
This your home now.
Ours ain't big enough
For you, me, and him
it never was.

As ZORA *passes* ANDRE *and places a hand on his
shoulder:*

(*To* ANDRE.) I'm sorry I saw it wrong.
But you wanted him.
He's yours for now.
But know that little spot you think you found won't ever fit
on you.
It'll always be too big.
Too wide.
(*To* FRANKLIN.) I love you times infinity.

ZORA *walks into the white room.* ANDRE *looks up and
follows her through the glass door and whispers something
in her ear. She looks up and whispers something to him.*

She leaves.

MAX *stands up and grabs* BELLAMY.

MAX (*to* BELLAMY). Let's go with Zora.

BELLAMY. I want to see what else he has to say.

FRANKLIN. You don't have to leave Max.

MAX (*ignoring* FRANKLIN). I know but I want to...
This place makes me feel gross.
I don't feel good here.

...

...

Like,
Here
You've me cast as a
supporting actor
in your narcissistic wet dream...
I'm done playing that role.
Let me know when you leave.
Bellamy I'm leaving.
You should too.

MAX *exits*. BELLAMY *looks after him and then back to* FRANKLIN.

BELLAMY (*to* FRANKLIN). I get it.
I –
I hurt a lot too.
Sometimes it feels better to be locked away
from the hurt.
Sitting on a hill
by a pool.
I don't blame you Franklin.
I think I just have to find my own hill.
My own pool, maybe.

She walks over and kisses FRANKLIN. *Then exits.*

FRANKLIN *stands in his Speedo and looks into the white room where* ANDRE *is standing and looking at the faceless white sculpture* FRANKLIN *made.*

FRANKLIN. So I guess it's just me and you. That's what we want though, right?

ANDRE. You didn't give me a face.

FRANKLIN....
It was hard for me to remember
what it, like

looked like?
In the light.

ANDRE. You didn't give me a face.

FRANKLIN. You said
you
that you wanted to see the world as I saw it.
I just / wanted

ANDRE. You knew the minute we met
that if you could get me, have me,
if I would have you,
that I would become worthless in your arms, didn't you?
That's why –
that's why you said
art was worthless
when it's owned
that was a warning wasn't it?
A warning.
A part of me always feared
that
you thought
I wanted to own you
that I wanted to make you worthless
because a part of me did.
and I thought you saw that part of me
who did want to have you,
Keep you
So you cast me as the villain
in this era of your life
and that was thrilling
because at least if I was the villain
I'd be remembered
you wouldn't forget my face
but no…
to you,
I wasn't even worth
attempting one.
I was ignorant.
Your mother was right.
Because you knew
you could carry my weight and toss it aside,

and rummage through what was left when it was all over,
right?
She's right.
(*A realization.*) I would never fit.
Can never.

FRANKLIN. What if that's true?

ANDRE. Are you not going to say?

FRANKLIN *looks back at him. As he's about to open his
mouth a phone begins to ring.*

Answer it.

A ring echoes throughout the theatre again.

FRANKLIN. No.

ANDRE *walks over and picks up the phone.*

ANDRE (*handing it to him*). Answer it.

…
It's him.
One villain without a face you've now modeled yours after.
It's him.
She told me it would be.
Answer it.

FRANKLIN *shakes his head no.*

ANDRE *looks at him as the phone continues to ring. He
takes a breath and exits. The phone continues to ring.*

FRANKLIN *looks at the house empty, sallow… his dolls
lying discarded upon the ground. He moves toward the Zora
and Franklin dolls and slowly places them beside each
other.*

FRANKLIN (*he sings some and speaks some… let him find it*).
    That's all you wanted.
    Someone special someone sacred,
    in your life…
    For just one moment.
    To be warm naked.
    At your side /
    Sometimes I feel like you'll never understand me.

He moves, away from the dolls and looks out at us.

BEEP!

(*Voice-over.*) Hi, you've reached Franklin.
Sorry I uh,
I can't get to the phone right now.
But if you need anything just leave a message
Or, like, send me an email
or a text
and I'll get back to you at my earliest convenience.
Um...
Thank you...

BEEP!

FRANKLIN *begins to slowly dance to the rhythm of the now cacophonous chorus of rings surrounding us. A slow, painful solo that moves like a serpent through his body.*

The chorus of ringtones continues as the lights from the still-boiling pool begin to blaze with intensity until all is blinding downstage, FRANKLIN *a black figure awash in white.*

I will be your father figure,
  put your tiny hand in mine
I will be your preacher teacher anything you had in mind,
  baby!

The song continues until we can take it no longer then:

End of play.